Romeo and Juliet

WILLIAM SHAKESPEARE

Guide written by

John Mahoney

A *Letts* EXPLORE **Literature Guide**

First published 1994
Reprinted 1998, 1999, 2000, 2002
This edition revised by Ron Simpson

Letts Educational
414 Chiswick High Road
London, W4 5TF
Telephone: 020 8996 3333

Text © John Mahoney

Series editor Ron Simpson

Typeset by Jordan Publishing Design

Text design Jonathan Barnard

Text illustrations Hugh Marshall

Cover illustration Ivan Allen

Design © Letts Educational Ltd

Acknowledgements
Outline answers are solely the responsibility of the author, and are not supplied
or approved by the Exam Board.

British Library Cataloguing in Publication Data
A CIP record for this book is available from the British Library

ISBN 1 85758 250 0

Printed and bound in Great Britain

Ashford Colour Press, Gosport, Hampshire

Letts Educational Ltd, a division of Granada Learning Ltd. Part of the Granada
Media Group.

visit www.letts–education.com for free education and revision advice.

Contents

■ Plot synopsis

The play is set mainly in Verona, a city in northern Italy. Romeo and Juliet are the children of two important families, the Montagues and the Capulets, who are engaged in an ancient feud.

The story begins with a street brawl with drawn swords between the servants of the two feuding families, which is brought to an end by the arrival of the Prince. He threatens the heads of both families with death if the disturbances do not stop.

Juliet's family, the Capulets, plan to marry her to Count Paris. At a masked ball given by the Capulets, Romeo and Juliet meet and fall in love. Juliet's cousin, Tybalt, recognises Romeo and has to be restrained from attacking him. Because of the enmity between their families, the lovers persuade a friendly priest, Friar Lawrence, to marry them in secret.

Romeo is accosted in the street by Tybalt, who challenges him to fight. For Juliet's sake Romeo declines. His friend Mercutio takes up the quarrel and is fatally stabbed. Romeo kills Tybalt in retaliation and is banished from Verona by the Prince.

Juliet's parents insist that her wedding to Paris should be brought forward. When she defies them, they threaten to disown her. She goes to Friar Lawrence for help. The priest tells her of a drug which will give her the appearance of death long enough to avoid marrying Paris. When it wears off, the Friar will take her to Romeo. Juliet takes the drug and is discovered in bed, apparently dead. She is put in the family vault.

Friar Lawrence tries to get word to Romeo, but his message is delayed. Romeo hears of Juliet's 'death' from another source. In despair he buys poison and returns to Verona. At Juliet's tomb he meets Paris who, taking him for a grave-desecrator, tries to stop him. They fight and Paris is killed.

Finding Juliet and believing her to be dead, Romeo takes the poison and dies by her side. Friar Lawrence arrives as Juliet wakes up to find Romeo's body. He panics and runs away. Juliet stabs herself with Romeo's dagger.

The play ends with the two grieving families vowing to be reconciled.

Romeo

At the beginning of the play Romeo is an immature and impulsive boy who imagines that he is in love with Rosaline. His talk is full of bookish and artificial expressions of emotion and he seems to be wallowing in self-pity. When he meets Juliet and falls in love with her, this has a dramatic effect on his character. He becomes more mature and even attempts to make peace with Tybalt, Juliet's argumentative and aggressive cousin. Despite his new-found maturity and tolerance of the Capulets, Romeo remains impetuous. He has one fixed idea (marriage to Juliet) and, within that, simply reacts to circumstances. He responds to plans thought up by others (Friar Lawrence, Juliet or the Nurse) and his mood swings from despair to joy, even within one scene, for example, Act 3, Scene 3.

Juliet

As with Romeo, once they have met, there is only one point of focus in Juliet's life. However, she is presented rather differently from Romeo as we see her much more in a convincing family situation where the coldness of her mother suggests why Juliet forms her opinions for herself. Despite her age, not quite fourteen, Juliet shows remarkable independence and maturity, but she is obedient to her parents until her love for Romeo makes such obedience impossible. She is intelligent and perceptive, possibly more so than Romeo. She is utterly loyal to Romeo and defies the whole world for him. She is prepared to risk taking a dangerous drug to fake death so that she can escape to be with him. She accepts death willingly at the end of the play, when fate has destroyed their lives.

The Nurse

The Nurse's position in the Capulet household is superior to that of a normal servant. Juliet seems to have taken the place of the daughter she once had, and everything she does, she does for Juliet's benefit. She is a simple soul who is an easy target for Mercutio's lewd ribbing. She is long-winded as well as rather rude and bawdy, but she seems sincere and makes the audience laugh with her rather than at her. The Nurse is Juliet's confidante and helper for much of the play, but forfeits her trust when she advises marriage to Paris after Romeo's banishment. Juliet is shocked both by her disloyalty to Romeo and her lack of moral sense in advocating a bigamous marriage.

The Friar

Friar Lawrence is a respectable and well-meaning ally of Romeo and Juliet. It is his plan which goes wrong and causes the final tragedy. He is a kindly but rather unworldly man who thinks himself careful and wise but who proves to be over-ambitious in his plans. His intentions seem good but he is too optimistic in hoping that the marriage of Romeo and Juliet will bring the two feuding families together. In the end it is their deaths which bring the Montagues and Capulets to their senses. At the end the Friar is revealed as a timid man when he runs away leaving Juliet alone in the tomb.

Lord Capulet

Capulet is a difficult character to assess because his behaviour seems so contradictory. He is a wealthy man who has married a woman much younger than himself, as she keeps reminding him. He presents an angry figure of short-tempered authority when Juliet refuses to obey him, but at other times speaks to her lovingly. He appears to think Juliet is too young to marry and tries to put Paris off when he asks for her hand. But later he suddenly agrees to the marriage and even brings the date forward, with disastrous results. He rages at Juliet when she shows reluctance to marry Paris and embodies the conventional, unfeeling world in which the lovers find themselves. Only at the end of the play, when he mourns for his daughter's death, does he seem a sympathetic character once more.

Lady Capulet

Lady Capulet has married a much older, wealthy man. She seems to think of marriage as a business which must be carefully planned to be profitable. She is unsympathetic and vindictive when she demands that Tybalt's killer be put to death. Lady Capulet does not seem to have a particularly affectionate relationship with her daughter, but leaves her to the Nurse. When Juliet appeals to her mother not to cast her out, her appeal falls on deaf ears.

Mercutio

Mercutio bursts onto the scene with his lively and bawdy wit. His brilliantly imaginative language contrasts sharply with that of his melancholy friend Romeo and the sensible Benvolio. Mercutio lives life to the full: he is witty, eloquent, loves to hear himself talk and does not suffer fools gladly. He seems to take neither life nor death very seriously. He is one of Shakespeare's most bawdy characters and his language contrasts with that of the maturing Romeo. His profane view of love emphasises the strength and purity of Romeo's mature love for Juliet. Mercutio is intensely loyal to Romeo and intervenes on his behalf against Tybalt with fatal results. His death launches the final tragedy of the play.

Paris

Paris is a character who is only lightly sketched in the play but who has an important role. He is an honourable man whose appearance helps to trigger the final tragedy. He confidently assumes that he will marry Juliet because this is the arrangement with her father Capulet. He is the embodiment of the predictable and conventional lover. At the end of the play this well-meaning man speaks delicate words of grief for the girl he hardly knew. It is his sense of honour, rather than any feelings of jealousy, that provokes outrage in him when he thinks Romeo has come to desecrate her tomb. He dies in the fight with Romeo without ever understanding the real situation.

Tybalt

Tybalt is the only member of the Capulet and Montague families whose words and actions show the ferocity and deep hatred associated with the feud: he attacks the peacemaker Benvolio in the first brawl, he attempts to challenge Romeo at the feast and, of course, his final conflict with Mercutio and Romeo is a pivotal point in the tragedy. Remember, though, that Tybalt is also spoken of with affection by Juliet and the Nurse.

Benvolio

Benvolio is a peacemaker and a contrast to the aggressive Tybalt. He is cautious, unlike Romeo. His word is trusted by both Montague and the Prince. He seems to be used as a contrast to the other characters in order to bring out their main features more clearly.

The Montagues

Montague and his wife remain thinly characterised and occupy predictable roles. Montague wishes to join in the first brawl, his wife dissuades him, then they make concerned enquiries about their melancholy son. Later they reflect the mood of the play by defending Romeo (very briefly) after the death of Tybalt and by sharing the grief at the end of the play, Lady Montague so acutely that she dies. Montague then joins in the final atonement and reconciliation.

Escalus, Prince of Verona

The Prince is a symbol of order and peace. He is an important figure because much of the play is about the clash between love and hate, youth and age, life and death. He speaks out against the family feud but is unable to stop it. In the end he admits that he should have been firmer, because it is the death of the lovers and not his authority that finally brings peace.

Themes and images in *Romeo and Juliet*

Themes are the important ideas that run through the play. You will come across them many times. They connect the story, the characters and the different scenes in the play.

When words and descriptions suggest a picture in your mind, that is called an image. Images are often used to make an idea stronger, or to encourage you to think of things from a particular point of view. If you described someone as being 'as thin as a rake' or as behaving 'like a wild animal' you would be using simple examples of images.

Disorder

Disorder

The play is full of examples of different kinds of disorder: brawls and fights, the violence of angry passion, the unnaturalness of infatuation or false love. The Prince threatens death at the start of the play; later Romeo dreams about his own death; death is constantly being predicted and five people actually die violently in the play. Dreams seem to be sent to torment us, as Mercutio says in Act 1, Sc 4 (his 'Queen Mab' speech). Imagery is used throughout the play to emphasise the danger of disorder. Look to see how images about the sea are used to suggest unpredictable danger. The disorder of life in Verona is also emphasised by the use of imagery to do with disease and sickness. This society is said to be filled with 'cankered hate', Romeo's sadness at the beginning is a 'madness' and a 'sickness' and his later love for Juliet needs the 'holy physic' (holy medicine) of the Friar. Images of sickness and disease in the play are often connected with plants and the world of nature.

Fate

Fate

Fate is an important theme in the play. From the very start Romeo and Juliet are described as 'star-crossed', or fated to disaster. Romeo says he feels his future is 'hanging in the stars' and that he is 'fortune's fool'. The overall structure of the play and the way the story unfolds produces a feeling of inevitability about the ending. Neither Romeo nor Juliet can ever really escape because, just when things look as though they might improve, some new disaster strikes.

Light and darkness

Light and darkness

Images of darkness in the play stand for death, violence, sadness and secrecy. At the start of the play Romeo seeks out darkness because he is sad and depressed. Later on he and Juliet welcome the night because then they can safely be alone in secret. At the end of the play the blackness of the tomb and the dark night outside emphasise the sadness and tragedy of the lovers' deaths.

Images of light, whiteness or paleness in the play often appear in connection with ideas of love, life and hope. Romeo describes Juliet as being like the sun, brighter than the light of a torch or the stars. Juliet talks about Romeo's love as pure — whiter than snow. Even in the darkness of the tomb at the end of the play Romeo says that Juliet's beauty makes the darkness light. Often the images of light and dark appear closely connected with images to do with the eyes, or with looking, sight or seeing.

Love and passion

Love and passion

The play is full of overflowing passions. At the beginning the servants seem to feel it is their duty to fight each other, so they fight for no other reason. Tybalt is always bursting with aggression and seems always determined to pick a fight. Even Romeo feels obliged to fight when his friend is killed. Capulet is violent in his language, as is Mercutio, except that in Mercutio's case the violence is a product of wild imagination rather than anger. The violence in the play is set against the peacefulness of the lovers when they are together.

Love is an important theme in the play and appears in many forms. Different characters talk about love from very different points of view. At the start the servants Sampson and Gregory see love as brutish and crude. Romeo's early sadness is a kind of intellectual love – he is in love with the idea of being in love. Mercutio and the Nurse talk about love from a very physical, bawdy point of view. At the other extreme, Lord and Lady Capulet see love merely as a financial transaction to do with securing and retaining wealth. The love between Romeo and Juliet is deep and passionate and is more powerful than hatred and even death.

Nature

Nature

At the time when Shakespeare wrote this play most people worked the land and gardens; orchards and woods figured more largely in their lives than today. Language and thought would probably revolve more around plants, animals and the seasons than today and the play is full of images drawn from nature, which reinforce or explain ideas about beauty and ugliness, health and sickness, things beneficial or things harmful. The Friar's speeches are full of such images but they also appear widely elsewhere. Images about animals are used in a similar way to those about plants. Beautiful or noble animals are like attractive or honourable people, whilst worms or reptiles suggest ideas about foul things in human life.

Time

Time

Time and the sense of time passing too quickly are ideas that are often repeated in the play. The speed with which events happen is an important factor in the tragedy.

At first time passes slowly, as Romeo frets about Rosaline and complains that the hours are long. Later Capulet complains that the years rush past too quickly. Romeo compares Juliet with a winged messenger of heaven, but Juliet worries that their love is too sudden and rash. The Friar complains that the lovers are in too much of a hurry. The message about the Friar's plan is delayed, and Friar Lawrence himself arrives at the end just seconds too late to stop the final tragedy. The whole play seems hurried.

Characters rush into marriage, Romeo is banished for an impulsive action, Capulet cannot wait to get Juliet married to Paris. The play is filled with speed – speed to kill whoever is in the way and speed to commit suicide when life seems empty. Everywhere there is angry feuding, surging passion and sudden death.

Essays

This icon is used throughout the **Text commentary** to draw attention to material that should be of particular relevance to the section **How to write a coursework essay**. Each time it is used, it is accompanied by a note that identifies which essay title the material relates to and adds a relevant comment, quotation or piece of advice.

■ Text commentary

Prologue

The Chorus tells the audience that the play will be about two lovers whose deaths will end the feud between their two families.

The Prologue features a device from ancient Greek drama (the Chorus) which Shakespeare uses rarely. The Greek Chorus was used to comment on the events in the play; here it gives the audience the facts of the feud and how the deaths of the lovers will end it. The ending is deliberately revealed so that the audience may judge characters and events in the light of the final tragedy and also to intensify the tragedy by making it seem inevitable. The Chorus emphasises that the lovers are fated. They are 'star-crossed', their love is 'death-marked' and they are born of their parents' 'fatal loins'.

Act 1 Scene 1

Servants from the two families of Capulet and Montague quarrel. Prince Escalus declares that he will punish further fighting with death. Romeo declares his love for Rosaline.

The play starts like a comedy, with word-play and puns from the two servants Gregory and Sampson, although they are armed and ready for trouble. Notice Sampson's one-dimensional idea of love as a kind of rape fantasy. He thinks love is just a matter of the brutal conquest of another's body, a matter of 'cutting off' a woman's virginity, and his imagery about the human body reflects this – it is vulgar and crude. For Sampson, even love has become a kind of hate.

The fighting begins

References to 'naked weapon' and 'tool' emphasise the physical side of love,

Time

as do other references to striking and thrusting. Amidst a whirl of this kind of talk, Sampson and Gregory meet their deadly enemies. The speed with which fighting breaks out prepares the audience for the way haste and speed play a big part in the coming tragedy. Many characters in the play seem to act first and think later. This quarrel begins almost as a farce; biting your thumb at someone is an ancient Italian insult.

We meet Benvolio and Tybalt

Benvolio's first words of 'Part, fools!' sum up his character. His name, roughly translated, means 'good will'. Equally, we meet Tybalt in characteristically aggressive mood. Tybalt's name comes from the old story of Reynard the Fox where Tybert is a cat (see also Act 2 Sc 4), hence our modern 'tibby'. Tybalt seems to hate hell, peace, Montagues – everything. His character never changes. He is always excitable and angry.

Characters

Before the main characters enter the culture of violence is established, and also the contrasting characters of two of the young men: Benvolio ('Put up thy sword') and Tybalt ('I hate hell, all Montagues and thee').

Capulet and Montague arrive

These two characters go through the motions of joining in the fight. Notice

how Lady Capulet deflates her foolish old husband – he calls for his sword and she suggests he'd be better off with a crutch. Equally, Lady Montague restrains her husband by holding on to him and scolding her. What impression do the heads of the two families make on their first appearance? Do you think they seem dangerous, or foolish, or both? Does this first scene suggest that the power of the older generation is handled wisely?

Prince Escalus appears and lays down the law

Escalus is furious with both families. He compares their behaviour to that of beasts. He says that there have already been three brawls and he has had enough. He is angry because their pointless fighting is disrupting the social life of the city and he threatens death to anyone who fights again.

Disorder

Key scene

Compare this scene with Act 3, Scene 1. In both scenes Tybalt is fighting a Montague when the older generation and the Prince arrive, either all together or immediately after each other. The difference is that this time they arrive before anyone has been killed.

Where is Romeo?

Characters have appeared in a careful order up to this point in the play. You have met Capulet's servants, Montague's servants, Benvolio, Tybalt, the

Capulets, the Montagues and then the Prince. The scene is set for the two main characters who have yet to appear.

Light and darkness

Benvolio becomes poetic when he talks about Romeo. Notice how the atmosphere of conflict suddenly disappears as Romeo is mentioned. Benvolio talks about sunlight, secrets and silence. These ideas and images accompany Romeo and Juliet throughout the play and you should keep an eye out for the consistent way they are used by Shakespeare to create a deliberate mood or atmosphere around the lovers.

Romeo is sick with love

Benvolio says that Romeo has been walking underneath a grove of sycamore

Romeo

trees. The name is probably being used as a pun: 'sick amour'. Plays on words and word–sounds are important in *Romeo and Juliet*. You should try to 'listen' in your mind to what the poetry sounds like, not just to catch the puns and clever use of words, but also to appreciate the way the sound of the words often supports or reinforces what is being said.

Fate

Romeo seeks out the darkness in his sadness. He is talked of as a fleeting shadow and is already being associated with speed and quickness. Similarly, notice how Montague talks about Aurora, the goddess of the dawn. Throughout the play you will find many references to mythology, the Bible and classical literature. These references are only connected with Romeo

or Juliet and serve to set their love story against the backdrop of superstition, great legends and the irresistible power of fate.

The imagery of 'the envious worm'

Montague says that he doesn't know why his son Romeo is so depressed. He

Disorder

says that his son is like a bud that has been secretly attacked inside by 'an envious worm' before it can open and show its sweet leaves to the air and its beauty to the sun. The worm is destructive and evil and envies the bud its beauty. This idea of the biting mouth of the worm destroying the bud's promise of beauty is an early use of an important theme that you will

find running through the play. By the end of the play the worms have become those of the grave and the biting mouth is death's mouth (the tomb) devouring Romeo and Juliet.

Confusion and chaos is everywhere

In Romeo's first long speech he talks about how love and hate have become mixed together, so that nothing is clear any more. Romeo's emotional and mental confusion is brought out in a series of oxymorons, that is to say,

Romeo

phrases made up of opposites. To begin with he talks of 'brawling love' and 'loving hate'. See how many more oxymorons you can find in this speech. These images of chaos and confusion are repeated often throughout the play, where life is seen as death and death as life. Just as the world of Verona is chaotic and confused because of the feuding families, so Romeo is confused because his feelings are in turmoil. Notice Romeo's mention of 'still-waking sleep, that is not what it is'; this is almost a vision of the future, where he will find Juliet seemingly dead.

Romeo's language

Romeo

Romeo's language is artificial, intellectual and rather forced. He uses so many ornate and different descriptions for his feelings because he is not really in love at all – he is in love with the idea of being in love. He talks a lot in rhyming couplets, which makes what he says sound more like a well-rehearsed speech than a true expression of emotional torment. Later when he meets Juliet, you will see how his language becomes more sincere and passionate. Romeo seems almost desperate to fall in love, but it is an idealised kind of love he wants; he is unrealistic, uncompromising and given to extremes, which helps to prepare us for his headlong fall into passionate love with Juliet.

Love
Romeo speaks in rhyming couplets of the charms of Rosaline. Compared to what he says later of Juliet, it seems very formal and generalised: 'O she is rich in beauty, only poor,/That when she dies, with beauty dies her store.'

Act 1 Scene 2

Paris seeks the hand of Juliet in marriage. Romeo learns that Rosaline is going to the banquet and decides to go also.

We meet Paris

The plot begins to develop some twists here. Paris wants to marry Juliet and

Paris

this will produce tragic complications for her and Romeo. Paris, unlike Romeo, is calm and even-tempered. Because of the family feud, Romeo cannot of course speak to Capulet when he falls in love with Juliet. Notice Paris' attitude to love – that a woman is fulfilled not by passion but by the calmer pleasures of motherhood.

About the imagery in the play

Juliet's 'ripeness' to be a bride is talked of in the same breath as summer

Nature

'withering'. Montague talks about Romeo being blighted like a bud bitten by a worm. These hints in the imagery prepare you for the tragedy to come. The love of Romeo and Juliet is full of promise and hope for the future but it will be blighted and doomed by fate. Capulet's other children have all died and the earth has 'swallowed' them. This is another example of the imagery of death's mouth (the tomb) in the play, which reminds you of the ever-present idea of the lovers as 'star-crossed' or fated.

Capulet says that at his banquet that night there will be many lovely young

Lord Capulet

women – 'earth-treading stars'. This connection between heavenly things and events on earth was a common idea in Shakespeare's time, and it is another example of the images of light and love being brought together. Other imagery that Capulet uses reinforces ideas that appear throughout the play. For example, he describes young women as 'fresh female buds'; throughout the play, youth and plants are related. Plants and youth are characterised by early and vigorous growth and are charming and innocent as they ripen. Old age is characterised by canker, infirmity, callousness, guilt and a lack of understanding.

Romeo and Benvolio find out about Capulet's feast

The comic servant, Peter, cannot read and so must get help to obey his master's instructions to find the people written on the list. Peter is described in the cast list as 'a clown' which means that the part was originally played by a member of the company who specialised in clowning and always played such parts. Though this is a very small part, we can find examples of typical clownish humour. One element of the humour is nonsense, muddling things in an illogical pattern. See what examples you can find of this in the short speech before the entry of Romeo and Benvolio. A pleasing variant on this is to use this nonsense to confuse intelligent people. Here you should note Peter scoring off Romeo by giving correct, but very limited, answers.

Romeo

Romeo and Benvolio speak to each other in verse while the servant speaks in prose, as fits his lower status. Notice that noble characters use prose when speaking to, or about, 'lower' things.

As you know already, the imagery in the play compares people with the plant and animal world. Benvolio says that if Romeo will go to Capulet's feast he will see Rosaline, whom he loves, but will also see many of Verona's other beautiful women. (Note that Rosaline is Capulet's 'fair niece'; Romeo has already fallen in love with a Capulet!) These

Nature

other 'admired beauties of Verona' will make Romeo think Rosaline is more like a crow than a swan. The elegant white swan is contrasted with the plain black crow, another reminder of the way black and white, light and dark, life and death are contrasted throughout the play. Notice how such images often appear together. Notice too that Benvolio's remarks prepare the audience for Romeo's first sight of Juliet at the feast by creating a sense of anticipation.

Romeo takes up the idea of light and seeing by saying that the 'all-seeing sun' never saw a beauty to match Rosaline. Later in the play – in Act 2 Sc 2

Light and darkness

– Romeo again uses the imagery of light and seeing to describe his love for Juliet, but she rejects it. Juliet says the light of the moon is not constant and their love may be more like a brief sudden flash of lightning. Notice how the speeches are full of references to light, burning, crystals, shining, eyes and looking. This continuous use of related images is part of the structure of the play and binds the different parts together.

Act 1 Scene 3

The Nurse reminisces about Juliet's childhood. Juliet learns about her father's plan for her to marry Paris.

Scenes 1 and 2 are about the world of men: Scene 3 concentrates on the world

Lady Capulet

as it affects women. The Nurse is informal and natural in her manner and speech, whilst Lady Capulet seems formal, abrupt and somewhat artificial. As with Romeo, Benvolio and the servant in the previous scene, the difference between the 'high' status of Lady Capulet and the 'low' one of the Nurse is reflected in the content and style of their speech.

The Nurse tells of Juliet's childhood

The Nurse's long speech here covers the whole life of the human body from Juliet's childhood to her own old age. The Nurse was Juliet's wet-nurse and she tells us how she persuaded the baby to give up feeding at the breast by rubbing wormwood (a bitter plant) on her nipples. The Nurse's daughter Susan died young and Juliet has in many ways replaced her in the Nurse's affections. Ironically, Juliet will also be 'too good for' the Nurse and this brief reference is ominous in the same way as Romeo's images of cankered buds. The Nurse has obviously had a long and close relationship with Juliet, which explains why Lady Capulet calls her back to join in the discussion about her proposed marriage to Paris.

The character of Nurse is based on the stock figure of the obscene old woman, a common character in the earlier plays of Shakespeare's time. Here

Shakespeare has given her the ironic name of Angelica (angel). The Nurse's language is full of very 'un-angelic' broad humour and sexual references. She recounts her husband's jest that Juliet (who had fallen on her face when small) would fall upon her back when she was older and wiser, i.e. that she would look forward to the pleasures of sexual intercourse.

About the structure of the play

The Nurse's bawdy jokes and her emphasis on physical lust act as an important balance to the later idealised and innocent love of Romeo and Juliet and to the formal and rather artificial love of Paris. Just as the Nurse is a balance to Juliet, so is Mercutio to Romeo. The whole of this amusing scene, in which the chatty and rambling Nurse keeps irritating Lady Capulet, is a temporary diversion from the tragedy to come. Scenes like this as 'light relief' from the impending disaster actually help to build tension because, whilst they seem to be about other things, they contain lots of cross-references to the main imagery and action. For example, Juliet is associated with 'falling backwards' (into physical love) and the matter of her possible marriage to Paris is raised. We know that these marriage proposals are about to be complicated by her falling in love with Romeo at the feast.

Lady Capulet's materialistic view of marriage

In keeping with her character in the rest of the play, Lady Capulet introduces the topic of marriage to Paris very abruptly and without much sensitivity. She expects Juliet to commit herself to someone she has not yet seen. Lady Capulet says Juliet could 'share all that he doth possess' and seems to see marriage as a sharing of position and wealth rather than a sharing of love. The Nurse agrees that Juliet could 'grow' by marrying Paris, but as usual has in mind a more bawdy meaning than Lady Capulet's! The imagery of sight and looking appears again as Juliet obediently says she will 'look to like'.

Act 1 Scene 4

On their way to the banquet Romeo's friends tease him because of his love for Rosaline.

Romeo's friends indulge in word-play about his love, saying that he should not be sad. Romeo is 'heavy' with sadness and has a 'soul of lead'; he has been pierced with Cupid's arrow. Although Romeo's bookish sadness will soon be lifted, his love for Juliet eventually brings more sadness by the end of the play.

We meet Mercutio

Mercutio is wild and fiery, volatile and impulsive. His words run away with

Mercutio

him in an almost uncontrollable flow and, in Act 2 Sc 4, Romeo says that Mercutio 'will speak more in a minute than he will stand to in a month'. The notion of romantic love amuses Mercutio, who has a much more vulgar and down-to-earth view of love which revolves around physical passion.

Disorder

Mercutio says that dreams are inhabited by the Fairy Queen Mab and that Romeo seems to have been enchanted by her. The dreams which Mercutio talks about are full of bizarre examples of wishful thinking: 'vain fantasies' as he calls them; Queen Mab drives her fairy coach through lovers' brains so that they dream of love, over ladies' lips so that they dream of kisses, over soldiers' necks so that they dream of cutting throats. In such dreams reality and madness seem to meet, and it is this sort of lovers' dream that is about to come true for Romeo.

Characters

Mercutio's Queen Mab speech is probably the most famous of the play not spoken by Romeo or Juliet. Despite his cynical air, it is full of fantastic imaginings and bizarre, but very precise, images. Typically of Mercutio, this speech is delivered in many different ways by actors. Can you compare different productions or films?

Romeo has a premonition

Romeo seems to foresee his own death here, a 'consequence yet hanging in

Fate

the stars' as he calls it. He calls upon the one 'that hath the steerage' of his 'course' – he who guides the path of his life – to direct him safely. The sea is often used by Shakespeare as a symbol of the powerful and unpredictable forces of fate and the audience already knows that Romeo's fate is fixed, for he is 'star-crossed'. This scene ends with a sense of foreboding but

Shakespeare uses the opening of the following scene to relieve the tension.

Act 1 Scene 5

Romeo sees Juliet at the banquet. Tybalt threatens to attack Romeo. Romeo and Juliet begin to fall in love and are dismayed when they discover their families are rivals.

The last scene ended on a gloomy and threatening note with Romeo having a premonition of his death. The opening of this scene is concerned with everyday domestic matters as the servants joke amongst themselves as they clear up after dinner.

Old age and youth

Capulet welcomes everybody and, although he is too old to dance himself,

he encourages everybody else to join in because he likes to watch the young people enjoy themselves. His speech is full of references to walking and dancing, and contrasts the hot vigour of youth with the sedateness of age, and its confusions. There are many references in the play to the brief joys of life and living and especially to the short-lived joys of the body, so soon overcome with stiffness, canker and decay. Many of the play's images emphasise the pleasures of growth and growing, food, sleep, exercise, lust, love, the promise of buds, the brief glory of flowers, the passing seasons and the sad inevitability of death.

Romeo first sees Juliet

Romeo sees Juliet and is stunned by her beauty. He associates her with

glowing light, says she shines like a rich jewel, compares her to a snowy dove amongst crows and says she is 'blessed'. As Benvolio said he would, Romeo now forswears his love for Rosaline at once. Near the start of Sc 2, Benvolio advised Romeo that, since one fire burns out another and one pain is made less by the anguish of another, he should therefore find a new love. This now happens, but we know that Romeo's pain will be made greater, not less, by his love for Juliet.

You will notice in the rest of the play how Romeo often talks about Juliet in terms of shining light, whiteness and purity, and as having holy qualities. He also says here that Juliet has beauty that is 'too rich for use' and is 'for earth too dear', meaning that she is too fine for the uses of this world and too precious to be on earth. This sounds rather ominous and again reinforces the sense of foreboding.

Tybalt first sees Romeo. Capulet reveals his true character

In contrast to Romeo's gentle and admiring love speech, Tybalt arrives, as usual spoiling for a fight. Capulet's banquet is a masked ball, so all the guests wear fancy masks to conceal their identity. This kind of ball was popular in Elizabethan times. Tybalt recognises Romeo's voice. He is furious that a Montague should intrude into their party and says he will fight Romeo for

this insult. Capulet tells him to calm down because Romeo is known to be virtuous and well-behaved. When Tybalt persists in wanting to kill Romeo because he is a Montague, Capulet becomes furious at his disobedience. You should consider how Shakespeare presents the character of Capulet. You might explain it in terms of the necessary action of the play: for the tragedy to occur he must be tolerant of Romeo here and intolerant of Juliet's wishes in Act 3. However, you will probably wish to find some consistency as well. What features of Capulet are the same when dealing with Tybalt here and with Juliet later? What is his attitude to family and feud? Is there ever any sign of personal animosity towards Romeo?

The lovers' first kiss

Love and passion

Romeo

Romeo and Juliet's speeches to each other are full of religious overtones, although the bulk of what they say concerns the human body. Although they talk of lips and hands kissing and touching, and actually kiss each other, they also talk about holy shrines, gentle sins, pilgrims, devotion, saints and prayers. Their formal use of language is rather dignified and stresses the purity and sincerity of their love for each other. Romeo's language is still a little forced and exaggerated and he has not yet completely shaken off his somewhat studied manner – Juliet says he kisses by the book rather than from the heart. The duet between Romeo and Juliet is in sonnet form and its use of religious words isolates the characters from the rest of the scene and its bustling activity.

Love
Though the Balcony Scene that soon follows is rightly famous, this first meeting marks out the love of Romeo and Juliet as something different. The text invites the producer to make the world literally 'stand still' around them, and the use of sonnet form is a bold device to emphasise devoted love which the Elizabethans would have recognised.

The verse in *Romeo and Juliet*

Mostly, Shakespeare's plays are written in a mixture of blank verse (regular, but unrhymed) and prose. However, *Romeo and Juliet* uses much more rhyme than most Shakespeare plays. You can find rhyming couplets (lines rhyming in pairs) used frequently: see what examples you can find in this scene. The most remarkable use Shakespeare makes of rhyme is to insert sonnets into the play. The sonnet is a form of romantic love poem which originated in Italy and was very popular in Elizabethan England. The speeches by Chorus as Prologues to Acts 1 and 2 are sonnets, and in this scene the first dialogue between Romeo and Juliet is in sonnet form.

The sonnet also uses iambic pentameter and has a very precise rhyme scheme. If you call the first rhyme sound 'A', the second rhyme sound 'B', and so on, the Shakespearean sonnet rhymes: ABAB, CDCD, EFEF, GG.

Love and passion

Starting from Romeo's, 'If I profane with my unworthiest hand', see if you can trace the sonnet form down to the final couplet spoken, one line each, by both lovers. You should be able to work out the effect of setting the opening dialogue of Romeo and Juliet in the most widely used form of love poetry.

The lovers discover each other's true identity

The Nurse brings a message that Juliet's mother wants her. Notice how when

The Nurse

the Nurse talks to Romeo she says that he who 'lays hold of her' will 'have the chinks' (be wealthy). Romeo has no interest in this – he is stunned to learn that Juliet is a Capulet, the family so bitterly at odds with his own. Juliet wants to know Romeo's name and asks the Nurse to find it out. She says that if she cannot marry Romeo she will die – another ominous comment. This is the first time in the play that death is portrayed as a bridegroom, although this image occurs again at the end. Juliet is distraught that she has found her only love within the family she has been brought up to hate. Compare the ways in which Romeo and Juliet discover each other's

Juliet

identity. In particular, note their very similar responses to the information. Juliet says that she met him and loved him before she knew who he was. This underlines the folly of the feud – if the two families would just accept each other as they are rather than as enemies, then the feud would disappear. Sometimes it is difficult to decide whether the play is more about the nature of hate than the nature of love, more concerned with death and darkness than with life and light.

■ Self-test questions Act One

Uncover the plot

Delete two of the three alternatives given, to find the correct plot. Beware possible misconceptions and muddles.

In Verona/Mantua/Rome, a fight between Montagues and Capulets is broken up by Benvolio/an Officer/the Prince. Romeo tells Benvolio/Tybalt/Mercutio the cause of his sadness: his love for Juliet/Angelica/Rosaline. Meanwhile, Tybalt/Paris/Balthasar asks Capulet for Juliet's hand. A Capulet servant, with supper invitations, seeks Romeo's help to find the houses/to identify the people/to read the list: Romeo decides to go to the feast for 'the admired beauties'/'the fair Rosaline'/'a cup of wine'. Lady Capulet/Lord Capulet/the Nurse tells Juliet about Paris – while outside, Romeo is teased by Benvolio/Tybalt/Mercutio. At the party, Tybalt/Capulet/Juliet recognises Romeo, but is restrained by Capulet/Mercutio/Benvolio. Romeo and Juliet meet – and part in shock: 'My only love sprung from a loathed enemy/a Capulet/my only hate!'

23

Who? What? Where? Why? How?

1 Who does Mercutio say gives dreams?
2 Who 'doth teach the torches to burn bright'?
3 What does Lady Capulet call for when Capulet calls for his sword?
4 What traditional Italian insult starts the brawl?
5 Where has Benvolio found Romeo walking before dawn?
6 Why (give three reasons) does Capulet restrain Tybalt at the feast?
7 Why can Romeo not have Rosaline?
8 How is Romeo recognised at the feast – and why is this the only way he can be recognised?
9 How many brawls have there already been between the families?
10 How many men does Juliet pretend to be interested in before she asks about Romeo?

Who said that?

1 Who says: 'Part, fools, put up your swords, you know not what you do'?
2 Who says: 'bright smoke, cold fire, sick health'?
3 Who agrees: 'True, I talk of dreams,/Which are the children of an idle brain'?
4 Who calls Romeo 'a virtuous and well-govern'd youth'?
5 Who shouts: 'What, drawn, and talk of peace? I hate the word!'?

Like what?

What do the following images describe?
1 'the bud bit with the envious worm'
2 'a snowy dove trooping with crows'
3 'earth-treading stars that make dark heaven light'
4 'a smoke rais'd with the fume of sighs'

What makes you think so?

Find four quotations (two statements and two hints) which tell you that Romeo and Juliet's love will end in death.

About time

1 How old is Juliet?
2 What time does Romeo return home from his brooding walks?
3 What 'lengthens Romeo's hours'?
4 What image does Mercutio use to show his impatience at delay?
5 Find two examples of the phrase 'too late' matched with 'too early'.

Whose side?

Identify which family (Montague or Capulet) the following belong to or are associated with.
Juliet, Romeo, Tybalt, Peter, Nurse, Sampson, Abraham, Gregory, Balthasar, Benvolio, Paris, Mercutio.

Act 2 Prologue

The Chorus says that the lovers cannot meet easily but that love will find a way.

Again the Chorus is used to keep the audience up to date with the story by summarising what has happened and by telling how the lovers' passion 'lends them power' to meet in the coming scenes, despite being enemies.

The Chorus speaks the third sonnet in the play, having started the play with the first. The second sonnet is spoken by Romeo and Juliet when they first meet.

Act 2 Scene 1

Romeo hides from his friends so that they go home from the feast without him.

Mercutio calls for Romeo, making bawdy fun of him because he is in love with Rosaline. Mercutio and his friends do not yet know that Romeo has met Juliet. Benvolio says that Romeo will be angry at being mocked this way.

Mercutio says Romeo is lusting after Rosaline

Love and passion

Mercutio

Mercutio talks about Cupid and Venus, two pagan symbols of love, but speaks about love in the most physical of terms, referring to Rosaline's 'scarlet lip' and 'quivering thigh'. Mercutio always talks about the human body, as he did in his Queen Mab speech, in very physical and bawdy terms. Here he says that Romeo will sit under a medlar tree. This is a piece of coarse Elizabethan slang; the medlar fruit, like a small brown apple, was said to resemble the female sex organs. This is why Mercutio says Romeo will think of Rosaline in these terms, because love for Mercutio is the same as physical lust. He and many other characters in the play cannot understand that love can be pure and passionate. The lovers are isolated because others do not understand their love.

Act 2 Scene 2

Juliet appears at a window above her garden and declares her love for Romeo. He reveals his presence to her and they exchange vows of love.

Romeo

Romeo, who has heard all these comments, remarks that Mercutio can easily make fun of him because Mercutio has never been in love; 'he jests at scars that never felt a wound'. The way in which Romeo expresses this is unintentionally ironic, because Mercutio is soon to be scarred and fatally wounded in his fight with Tybalt.

Romeo sees Juliet at her balcony

Light and darkness

The play is full of commotion and activity. Very rarely do we find a scene set in stillness: here, perhaps briefly at the start of Act 3, Scene 5 and, of course, finally in the silence of the tomb. Imagery of light and seeing is important in this scene. Romeo's love for Juliet is often expressed in terms of light shining within the darkness. Light imagery reaches its climax in this love scene, when he says that she is the source of all light, the sun.
Romeo connects the pale moonlight with sickness and grief and says that only fools have anything to do with it. This echoes the 'sick amour' he

Juliet

experienced at the start of the play when he was foolishly in love with Rosaline. He says the moon is 'envious' of the light of the sun and is 'sick and green'. Romeo's speech in praise of Juliet describes the beauty of the light of the sun and the other stars. Later, he speaks of her as a 'bright angel' who, as a 'winged messenger of heaven', is far above ordinary mortals on earth. Romeo uses several religious references to describe Juliet, indicating the kind of love he feels for her.

'O Romeo, Romeo, wherefore art thou Romeo?'

Love and passion

Juliet

The love scenes are separated from the rest of the play in different ways. For example, this scene is physically separated from the rest of the play by being set in a moonlit garden. The lovers exist outside the feuding and quarrelling. Their love is shown as eternal and pure, rather than motivated by physical desire, lust or money-grabbing. This is reflected in the kind of language and imagery that the lovers use.

Juliet, unaware that Romeo is hiding below in the garden, says that she does not care that he is a Montague. She says that if a rose were called by a different name it would still smell as sweet. Notice that Juliet uses an image of a beautiful flower to talk about Romeo. Her description of her ears drinking in his words shows that all her senses are awakened by her love for him and introduces imagery of mouths, drinking, etc.

Love

You must use quotations from this scene in any essay on love. Note in particular the way in which Romeo and Juliet at once put the family feud aside as less important than their love: 'I'll no longer be a Capulet' (Juliet)/'Call me but "love", and I'll be new baptized' (Romeo).

'For stony limits cannot hold love out'

Juliet is worried that Romeo risks death if he is discovered in her garden and

Romeo

wonders how he climbed the high orchard walls. He replies that love enabled him to climb the walls so easily. The 'stony limits' of Juliet's orchard, which Romeo says cannot hold out his love, also appear again at the end of the play, where they become the stony limits of the graveyard and the tomb. Romeo's love for Juliet becomes so strong that not even death can keep them apart. He says that love fears nothing, preparing us for the desperate measures which Juliet takes later to avoid marrying Paris.

Romeo says he would rather die than be without Juliet's love

Romeo unwittingly foretells his own death. He says he would rather have his

Romeo

life ended quickly by being found here in the garden by Juliet's kinsmen – 'ended by their hate', as he puts it – than die of slow suffering without Juliet's love. Because the audience already knows how the story will end, this comment by Romeo is a piece of dramatic irony. Dramatic irony occurs when a character's understanding of the situation or of future events is different from (usually opposite to) what the audience knows to be true.

The gods laugh at lovers' promises, says Juliet, because they are often wrapped up in deceitful language. She says that she will 'frown and be perverse' and refuse his affections if he dislikes her yielding too quickly.

'O swear not by the moon, th'inconstant moon'

Romeo used imagery about light when describing his love for Rosaline and

Juliet

now he tries to use the moon to evoke his love for Juliet. Continuing her words about being truthful, she says she does not want him to swear by the 'inconstant' (not constant) moon. The moon's light is not constant because it waxes and wanes throughout the year – sometimes it is strong and at others it disappears.

Juliet says their love is too like a flash of lightning

Light and darkness

Romeo is intoxicated by his passion for Juliet but she says 'it is too rash, too unadvis'd, too sudden', like the lightning in a storm. In a way Juliet is correct, because their love will indeed be like a brief wondrous flash of light in the darkness of the feud between their two families. This is another example of dramatic irony. It is also another example of the many images of light and shining which fill this scene.

Time

Juliet is afraid of being 'quickly won'. Time and the sense of time passing quickly are ideas that are repeated often in the play, where the action takes place in a very short space of time – this point, for example, marks the end of the first day.

Imagery of nature, buds and flowers

Nature

Notice the imagery of growth in Juliet's words: their 'bud of love' may become a 'beauteous flower' when they next meet, if it is breathed upon by 'summer's ripening breath'. References to nature tell you that their love is as natural as the seasons, and as innocent and beautiful as a flowering bud. Notice that their love has not yet fully flowered and that the ending of the story will prevent this. Also, the natural development of bud to flower is completed in the natural cycle of death and decay and the play has already prepared us for this with images like the worm in the bud.

'O blessed, blessed night'

Juliet

Romeo is afraid that his wonderful meeting with Juliet has been only a dream. Notice how it is she who returns with practical plans for seeing each other again and for arranging to be married. What do you think is the dramatic effect of Juliet's exits and entrances prompted by the Nurse's cries and her desire to speak to Romeo? She uses imagery of birds and flight – swiftness and flight will shortly become important in the action. Ominously, she also says that if Romeo were a bird she would kill him 'with much cherishing': dramatic irony again.

Light and darkness

This scene opened with Romeo comparing Juliet to the sun and stars and ends with the real dawn arriving as the lovers part. Many symmetries like this occur in the play revealing its skilful construction. The imagery is used both poetically, to emphasise what is meant, and structurally, to bind the action and themes of the play together. Notice the way the beautiful imagery of night being chased away by dawn describes darkness as 'a drunkard' who reels (sways dizzily) away from the pathway made by Titan's wheels. The Titans were the earliest gods in Greek mythology and one of them (Hyperion) was the father of the sun and the moon and dawn; he drove his chariot across the sky and in this image darkness reels away from his swift chariot. The image anticipates a later speech by Juliet ('Gallop apace, you fiery-footed steeds...' Act 3, Scene 2) and prepares us for the entry of the Friar in the next scene.

You may, in fact, find that in your edition, the four lines from 'The gray-eyed morn...' to 'Titan's burning wheels' are given to Friar Lawrence at the beginning of the next scene. The original text repeated the lines and editors have to decide where Shakespeare wished to place them. This shows the difficulty in editing the plays, but also shows how the imagery links together the scenes.

Act 2 Scene 3

Romeo meets Friar Lawrence and he agrees to help Romeo marry Juliet.

The Friar

The Friar is the last of the important characters to appear. Much of his speech is in rhyme and although rhyme is often used in the play it is never used in such concentration as here. This helps set off the Friar from the other characters.

The Friar is introduced to us in this long speech which is in some ways equivalent to Mercutio's Queen Mab speech in

Nature

Act 1 Sc 4. The Friar says the earth is both nature's womb and her tomb and that people are nature's children, who suck on her 'natural bosom', meaning that they are nourished by the natural world. He says that the plants he gathers contain reviving medicine as well as poison and that even the most vile things produce some good. This would be understood by a perceptive audience to be a double reference: the way the love of Romeo and Juliet can spring from the hatred of their families; and the way their deaths will end the feud.

Love and passion

He also says that people are like plants and have both good and evil in them. The good in man he says is 'grace', meaning graciousness or divine virtue. The evil in man he says is 'rude will' meaning fleshly desire or uncontrolled passion. You should by now be able to place several characters in each of these two categories. This idea, that too much will or passion can turn to vice, is an underlying theme in the play and one which the friar is always repeating. Just as the Friar mentions poison, the future victim of poison, Romeo, enters.

Romeo tells the Friar that he loves Juliet

Romeo

Romeo says that he has been 'wounded' by Juliet but that the Friar has medicine ('physic') that can cure him. This is ironic because although Romeo means that he has fallen in love with Juliet and the Friar can marry them, in the end it is the Friar's potion for Juliet that has disastrous consequences. Following on from the Friar, Romeo's speech combines the imagery of food, love-sickness and medicine.

The Friar is amazed that Romeo has fallen out of love and in again so quickly, but he agrees to help him

The Friar

The Friar's remarks here are very observant. Notice how he says that young men's love lies in their eyes and consider the way all the imagery of light, sight and seeing is used in the play. The Friar saw that Romeo's feelings for Rosaline were only infatuation and says that Rosaline herself knew this too. The imagery of 'burying' love in a grave sounds an ominous note.

Act 2 Scene 4

Tybalt challenges Romeo to a duel. Romeo sends a message to Juliet about their secret marriage plans.

Mercutio believes that Romeo has stayed out all night because of his love-sickness for Rosaline. Benvolio says that Tybalt has written a letter challenging

Romeo to a duel. Mercutio replies that Romeo is as good as dead already through love and in no state to fight. Ironically this is true, but not in the way Mercutio means.

Mercutio mocks Tybalt's fencing skills

Here Mercutio ridicules the new fashion for the Italian style of fencing that was much scorned in England at this time because of its precise, almost dance-like, technique. He says that such fencing is too much 'by th' book', like Romeo's kissing. Fancy speech or manners – or fencing as here – are again equated with falseness and shallowness.

'Here comes Romeo, here comes Romeo!'

Mercutio greets Romeo's entrance with another bout of bawdy punning in

which Romeo joins. Eventually Mercutio cries for Benvolio to separate them in their duel of words. Later, Romeo's love for his friend produces disaster when he separates Tybalt and Mercutio. The verbal duelling between Romeo and Mercutio prepares us for a different kind of duelling later. The comic elements of this scene create a change of atmosphere from the last scene and a contrast with the next.

Characters

The exchange between Mercutio and the Nurse is interesting from a number of angles. How offensive is Mercutio? Perhaps one's opinion is coloured by whether his humour still seems amusing. How offended is the Nurse in reality? Most convincing is Benvolio's behaviour: he joins in with one mildly rude joke and leaves the rest to the 'saucy merchant' Mercutio.

Mercutio and Benvolio make fun of the Nurse and Mercutio dominates the first half of this scene with Romeo, just as the Nurse dominates the second. Romeo's comment about Mercutio after he has left ('...loves to hear himself talk...') applies equally to the Nurse, and in some ways she and Mercutio are parallel characters: they are both bawdy and talkative and they both see life and its pleasures in purely physical terms.

Romeo arranges for the Nurse to tell Juliet of the elopement plans. The Nurse tells Romeo about Paris

The comic conversation with the Nurse, who often speaks more than she listens, tells us how she is to help with the elopement by lowering a rope ladder

The Nurse

from Juliet's room for Romeo. Romeo imparts his message to the Nurse with some difficulty. See how many examples you can find of the Nurse changing the subject, failing to listen to the end of an instruction or simply pursuing her own conversational interests. Her question about Romeo and rosemary beginning with a letter (followed by her confusion of 'r' and a dog growling) suggests her illiteracy.

'Doth not rosemary and Romeo begin both with a letter?'

The Friar

The Nurse here connects rosemary with Romeo and says that Juliet is fond of both. Later, after the discovery of Juliet's body, the Friar mentions rosemary in connection with Juliet. Later still the Nurse casts rosemary on the body of Juliet, as the flower of remembrance, and this reference would therefore have had a threatening ring for Elizabethan audiences.

Act 2 Scene 5

The Nurse gives the message to the anxious Juliet.

Time

Juliet is anxious to know why the Nurse has been so long. She says love's messengers should travel as fast as the sun flickers when clouds blow over it. This image connects the themes of haste and light and reminds us of Juliet's observation that some forms of love appear and disappear as quickly as lightning. This scene emphasises another theme: the contrast between the impatience of youth and the slowness of age; the blood rushes to Juliet's cheeks but the Nurse has a headache and an aching back.

More about age and youth

The Nurse

This scene between Juliet and the Nurse parallels the one in Act 2 Sc 3 between Romeo and the Friar. Both conversations show youth contrasted with age. The Friar's attitude makes him appear wise and kindly, but the Nurse is content for Juliet to be happy and shares the anticipation of the sexual pleasures of her wedding bed that night ('you shall bear the burden soon at night'). The Nurse's summary of Romeo is full of physical description – his face, his leg, his hand, foot and body – echoing Mercutio's earlier description of Rosaline. The Nurse is like Mercutio in the way she concentrates on the physical and often sexual side of life.

Act 2 Scene 6

Juliet meets Romeo in Friar Lawrence's cell. The Friar prepares to marry them.

The Friar

The Friar talks about the marriage of Romeo and Juliet and says the heavens will 'smile' on it. A few lines further on Romeo defies 'love-devouring death' to do whatever it dares. By the end of the play the mouth-imagery has turned from smiling heaven to the devouring mouth of the tomb.

'These violent delights have violent ends'

The Friar

The Friar delivers his usual lecture about how the excess of any passion will lead to tragedy. What he says is prophetic, considering what fate has in store for the two lovers. Notice his warning that 'violent delights have violent ends' and that they are like 'fire and powder' (meaning gunpowder) because when they meet they destroy each other; 'as they kiss consume'. This prophetic remark applies both to the feud – Tybalt and Mercutio will both die violently – and to the passion of the lovers.

'Too swift arrives as tardy as too slow'

By this confusing remark the Friar means that people should love moderately,

Time

not with too much haste and passion (too swiftly) nor with too little interest or emotion (too slow). This is true on two separate occasions in the play: first, when the Friar's message to Romeo is delayed and Romeo buys poison in his ignorance of the plan to fake Juliet's death; second, when Romeo arrives at the tomb before Juliet has awoken from her mock-death and takes the poison before the Friar arrives to tell him the truth.

Love

Many wise comments come from Friar Lawrence: on religion, 'So smile the heavens upon this holy act'; on moderation, 'Therefore love moderately, long love doth so.' Compare his words with his deeds.

■ Self-test questions Act Two

Uncover the plot
Delete two of the three alternatives given, to find the correct plot. Beware possible misconceptions and muddles.

Benvolio and Mercutio seek Romeo/Rosaline/Tybalt. Juliet declares her love for Romeo, who reveals himself, saying: 'I'll take thee at thy word'/'Shall I hear more?'/'If my heart's dear love –'. Juliet is afraid that he will fall from the high wall/that her kinsmen will kill him/that he will get lost. They exchange vows. Romeo goes to Friar Lawrence, who is seen planting herbs/putting plants in a basket/mixing medicines. He agrees to marry them because it may end the feud/because of Romeo's tears/because 'women may fall'. Meanwhile, Benvolio/Mercutio/Tybalt has challenged Romeo to a duel. After much banter, Romeo tells Peter/Benvolio/the Nurse of his plan to marry Juliet and send a ring/rope/rope ladder to reach her later. Told the news in her turn, Juliet jumps/blushes/faints. The lovers meet at the church/the orchard/the Friar's cell.

Who? What? Where? Why? How?
1   Who is 'the courageous captain of compliments'?
2   Who is 'a gentleman... that loves to hear himself talk'?
3   What two solutions does Juliet see to the problem of Romeo's identity?
4   What 'cannot hold love out'?
5   What does 'wherefore' mean (as in 'wherefore art thou Romeo?')?
6   What does Juliet ask Romeo to swear by – and not to swear by?
7   Where is Juliet supposed to be going when she leaves to marry Romeo?
8   Where does the 'balcony scene' take place?
9   Why has Friar Lawrence chided Romeo?
10 How does Tybalt fight, according to Mercutio?

Who said that?
1   Who says: 'My bounty is as boundless as the sea,/My love as deep'?
2   Who says: 'The earth that's nature's mother is her tomb'?
3   Who says: 'The pox of such antic, lisping, affecting fantasticoes!'?
4   Who says: 'Then love-devouring death do what he dare./It is enough I may but call her mine.'?
5   Who says: 'But you shall bear the burden soon at night'?

Open quotes
Find the line – and complete the phrase or sentence.
1   'But passion lends them power...'
2   'But soft! What light through yonder window breaks?...'
3   'For this alliance may so happy prove...'
4   'Had she affections and warm youthful blood...'
5   'These violent delights...'

About time
1   Why does Juliet 'have no joy of this contract tonight'?
2   What are Friar Lawrence's two proverbs or sayings about the results of haste?
3   When is Juliet to send to Romeo for news, and how long will it seem to her?
4   How long is the Nurse supposed to be away, and how long does she take?

Looking forward to the end?
For each of the following quotes, what is being talked about in the present – and why does it sound ominous, if you know what happens later in the play?
1   'He jests at scars that never felt a wound.'
2   'My life were better ended by their hate/Than death prorogued wanting of thy love.'
3   'Yet I should kill thee with much cherishing.'
4   'And bad'st me bury love'. 'Not in a grave.'
5   'Come between us, good Benvolio.'
6   'But old folks – many feign as they were dead.'
7   'Therefore love moderately: long love doth so.'

Act 3 Scene 1

Mercutio picks a fight with Tybalt, who wants to fight Romeo instead. Romeo tries to prevent the fight but Mercutio is killed. Romeo kills Tybalt, then escapes. Prince Escalus banishes Romeo from Verona.

This scene marks the final appearance of Mercutio. After this, our attention

Mercutio

is concentrated only on Romeo and Juliet. Unusually for Shakespeare, *Romeo and Juliet* has no subplot at all, and the simple and clear storyline which results gives the play a relentless feeling.

This scene is a major turning-point in the play and it is appropriate that it should start with references to heat and passion.

Benvolio advises Mercutio to be careful

Love and passion

As usual the peace-loving Benvolio is all for caution. He says to Mercutio that the day is too hot, members of the Capulet family are about and they should leave. Mercutio replies that this is poor advice coming from someone as hot-tempered as Benvolio. This is comic because the only person more inclined to fight than Mercutio is Tybalt, whereas Benvolio is a natural peacemaker.

Tybalt and Mercutio quarrel

Disorder

The exchange of insults between Mercutio and Tybalt shows how both of them will pick a fight over nothing. Benvolio warns them that they are in a public place where 'all eyes gaze on us' but they seem not to care. In any case, Tybalt is more interested in quarrelling with Romeo, who enters at this point.

Romeo will not fight with Tybalt

Romeo

The audience knows that Romeo has just married Juliet. Because Juliet is Tybalt's cousin, Romeo will not fight someone who is now a member of his own family. Tybalt does not know any of this, of course, and so he can't understand why Romeo will not be provoked into a fight. Mercutio is disgusted at Romeo and thinks that he is submitting to Tybalt's insults in a shameful way.

'A plague o' both your houses'

Mercutio fights with Tybalt but is fatally wounded as Romeo steps between them to try to stop them. Mercutio's insults to Tybalt revolve around his name. The animal imagery of 'rat-catcher' and 'king of cats' is continued as Mercutio

Nature

threatens to take one of Tybalt's 'nine lives', and becomes ironic as he describes his fatal wound as 'a scratch'. Even as he lies fatally wounded, Mercutio's language is full of humour. He says his wound is not as 'deep as a well' nor as 'wide as a church door', but it is enough. He is also talking about his own funeral and his burial. He tells Romeo that if he asks for him tomorrow he will find him 'a grave man', meaning he will not be making any more jokes because he will be in his grave. Mercutio leaves the scene, cursing both 'houses' and wishing a plague on both Capulets and Montagues.

Characters

Mercutio and Tybalt die. Tybalt's motives and character are, as always, absolutely clear: he wants to fight Montagues and, failing that, will fight with a Montague's friend. Mercutio's feelings are less obvious. He challenges Tybalt: loyalty to Romeo, sense of honour or sheer hot-headedness? He dies with wit and satire: bitter, or noble, or devil-may-care?

'O Romeo, Romeo, brave Mercutio is dead'

Romeo

Romeo blames himself for his friend's death, so when Tybalt returns he vows to show 'fire-ey'd fury' towards him. Romeo and Tybalt fight, and Tybalt is killed. Benvolio says that Romeo must escape quickly before he is caught, otherwise he will be subject to the death penalty as Prince Escalus warned at the start of the play. Romeo says he is 'fortune's fool', then leaves.

Romeo sees the trap he is caught in. If he escapes, he must leave his wife Juliet. If he stays, he risks the death penalty for brawling in the streets. He has ended up losing his best friend Mercutio and killing his wife's cousin.

Prince Escalus hears about the fight and Romeo is banished

Lady Capulet

Benvolio tells the Prince about the fight. Lady Capulet takes up the violent theme of the feud and demands that Romeo be put to death in punishment. She is a good example of how single-mindedness and anger can prevent people from being civilised and tolerant. This is a message constantly found in the play. The Prince banishes Romeo from Verona.

Focus on the lovers

The end of this scene is approximately the half-way point in the play, and the second half will prove very different from the first. Mercutio and the Nurse have been prominent and interesting characters, not rivalling Romeo and Juliet in terms of audience sympathy, but making a notable contribution to both comedy and drama.

Key scene

This scene divides the play in so many ways that it could be described as the pivot of the drama. The balance between tragedy and comedy is disturbed; the focus on characters changes; the mood shifts abruptly; this is a major turning point in the plot.

Now, as the action focuses even more strongly on the tragic love story, comedy virtually disappears from the play. Mercutio is dead and, after her betrayal of Juliet later in the act, the Nurse plays a much less important role.

Tybalt is now dead and Benvolio disappears from the action. In this scene the ever-reliable Benvolio acts as a Chorus to clarify matters. His purpose in the play is now over and he is seen no more. He has acted as a peacemaker, a contrast to Mercutio and Tybalt, and a social companion for Romeo, all roles that are no longer in the play.

The emphasis in the second half of the play is totally on Romeo and Juliet

Love and passion

and their ill-fated love. No major scene takes place without one of them present, though Juliet spends the later stages of Act 4 apparently dead. Of course, the tragic turn of the plot means that their scenes together are few in number. Check through the remaining scenes of the play to find out how much time Romeo and Juliet will spend together now that the death of Tybalt has ruined their hopes.

Act 3 Scene 2

Juliet learns of Tybalt's death and Romeo's banishment.

Events begin to move more quickly now and, even as Romeo's banishment is still ringing in your ears, you meet Juliet here longing for Romeo. Putting two such different things together produces a powerful dramatic contrast.

Juliet wishes that night would come quickly

It is appropriate that Juliet's long soliloquy, spoken in beautiful poetry, should

Time

begin with images of galloping horses, fire and speed. Phaeton, whom Juliet mentions, is a character from mythology, the son of Phoebus the sun-god, who almost destroyed the universe by recklessly driving the sun's fiery chariot too close to earth. Juliet calls upon Phoebus to bring night quickly so that she can secretly meet Romeo.

'Give me my Romeo; and when I shall die...'

Juliet is wishing for Romeo so that they can be together and share the pleasures of sexual love, and the references to death also contain the

Juliet

Elizabethan meaning of sexual ecstasy. Juliet says that if she may have Romeo until she 'dies' then she will share him with all the world as many 'little stars' that will put the light of the sun to shame. This use of star imagery echoes that used by Romeo in his first speech in the balcony scene in Act 2 Sc 2. Notice how in both speeches it is the pure and innocent nature of the light that is stressed in the imagery, but how death is also part of the imagery in Juliet's speech here.

The Nurse brings Juliet the news of Tybalt's death and Romeo's banishment

Disorder

The confusion in the Nurse's speech makes it difficult for Juliet to know at once what the bad news is. Juliet asks the Nurse 'what storm is this that blows so contrary?' because of the seeming contradictions in what the Nurse is saying. The imagery of violence and storms follows the lovers through the play.

In Act 2, Scene 5, just as here, an impatient soliloquy by Juliet is followed by an urgent message from the Nurse which takes a long time to deliver. See what similarities and differences you can find between the scenes: you might look at Juliet's mood at first, the atmosphere of the scene with the Nurse and the reasons why the Nurse takes so long conveying her meaning.

Key scene

Shakespeare uses the same format in three important scenes. Juliet, alone or with Romeo, speaks glowingly of love and looks forward anxiously or eagerly. The Nurse then brings important news. The last of these scenes is Act 3, Scene 5, in which the Nurse's news leads to a major confrontation between Juliet and her parents and, finally, her total isolation.

Nature

When Juliet is finally told about the events that have happened, she curses Romeo: 'O serpent heart, hid with a flowering face...'. This speech is filled with the contrasting use of opposites (oxymorons), like Romeo's speech at the start of the play ('bright smoke, cold fire...'). Concentrated in both speeches you will find many of the references which are scattered throughout the rest of the play. Notice, for example, the use of creatures like the serpent, raven and wolf to suggest dark and dangerous qualities.

'Blister'd be thy tongue'

Juliet's anger at the Nurse's criticism of Romeo shows her loyalty to Romeo and she quickly recovers from her initial reaction to Tybalt's death.

Juliet

Undoubtedly this change of attitude to Romeo is partly a reaction to the Nurse's words, 'Shame come to Romeo.' It is one thing to bemoan the fact that beauty and evil can coexist, another to curse her husband. What other reasons can you find for Juliet's first response and for her change of mind? She gives at least three reasons in defence of Romeo.

The imagery of death as Juliet's lover

Juliet's reaction to Romeo's banishment is significant. She says that Romeo's

Love and passion

banishment has killed everything: 'father, mother, Tybalt, Romeo, Juliet' and that there 'is no end, no limit, measure, bound, in that word's death.' She says that this sad news has removed all joy from her life. Notice how she says that death, not Romeo, will take her maidenhead (her virginity). This idea is taken up again at the beginning of the next scene. The suggestion throughout is that both she and Romeo are in a way already 'dead' because they will be separated by banishment.

Act 3 Scene 3

The Friar arranges for Romeo to escape to Mantua. Romeo goes to see Juliet.

Romeo has hidden at Friar Lawrence's cell. The Friar comes to tell him that

The Friar

his punishment is not death but banishment. This is an ironic twist to the story because the audience knows that this will be reversed at the end of the play. Notice how the Friar also uses the imagery of death as a lover, which Juliet also used at the end of the last scene, when he says that Romeo is 'wedded to calamity'. This reinforces what the Chorus said about the lovers being 'star-crossed'. The image of death as a lover appears again more strongly in the tomb at the end of the play. The Friar tells Romeo that he should be patient and accept the sentence of Prince Escalus.

'There is no world without Verona's walls'

Romeo

Romeo says that to be banished is as bad as being condemned to death because his whole world (Juliet) is in Verona. The Friar tries to persuade him that the Prince has been very merciful, but Romeo is beyond listening. Romeo says that cats, dogs, mice and 'every unworthy thing' will be able to 'live in heaven' because they can see Juliet, but he will not. Look carefully at the part of Romeo's speech here where he talks about poison: 'Hast thou no poison mix'd...'. Romeo is asking the Friar whether he has no other sudden means of death to kill him, as this would be kinder than the word 'banished', which Romeo says is a word which the damned use in hell. The use of potions and poisons is of course an important part of the tragedy and it is connected here with the Friar and later with the apothecary whom Romeo goes to see in Mantua.

More about the themes of youth and old age

The theme of the inability of old age to understand the feelings of the young

Disorder

occurs again in Romeo's speech to the Friar, beginning: 'Thou canst not speak of that thou dost not feel'. It is very like his comment that Mercutio could joke about being in love because he had never felt it himself. These sentiments emphasise the gulf between the world of the lovers and that of the other characters in the play. Juliet is equally frustrated with the Nurse at the end of this act, because she cannot understand Juliet's impatience or her depth of feeling for Romeo. The common bond between the Friar and the Nurse is their relationship with Romeo and Juliet.

The Nurse comes to the Friar's cell

Love and passion

The Nurse arrives to tell Romeo of Juliet's dismay at the news. Romeo again blames himself for events. He asks the Friar to tell him in which part of his body his name lives so that he might cut it out. This is an interesting contrast to Juliet's speech about Romeo's name in Act 2 Sc 2: 'Tis but thy name that is my enemy...'. This is another example of the play's theme of outside appearance as contrasted with inner reality.

'Art thou a man?'

The Friar's long, calm speech here slows down the pace of the action. What

The Friar

he says in this scene is important to the plot and it summarises the basic themes of the play. He says Romeo is behaving like a wild animal, instead of a man, by letting his emotions get the better of him. He tells Romeo that he has everything to live for and he should count his blessings: Juliet is alive, Tybalt, who wanted to kill him, is dead, and the law – which said he should be executed – has instead said he must only be exiled. Note the Nurse's response to the Friar's speech: 'O Lord, I could have stayed here all the night/To hear good counsel'. How much does she learn from the Friar's words? Compare the 'good counsel' (advice) she gives Juliet in Act 3, Scene 5. Friar Lawrence tells Romeo to go to Juliet and comfort her and then to leave for Mantua before daybreak. The Friar says he will find a way to let everyone know about their marriage, return them to their friends and beg a pardon from the Prince, after which Romeo will be able to return. Romeo is won over by the Friar's reassurance and all seems well until the next scene, when a new twist of fate drives the action towards the tragic conclusion.

Act 3 Scene 4

Capulet announces that he wants Juliet to marry Paris in three days' time.

Capulet is talking to his guest Paris late on Monday night. He seems to have taken the death of Tybalt with surprising calm. He tells him that Juliet is distraught but that he will speak to her and that he intends the wedding to be brought forward to Thursday. Capulet stresses that it will have to be quiet out of respect to Tybalt's memory. Capulet gives no reason for this sudden change of mind, nor for the sudden haste. The main hint of a changed situation is Juliet's grief which, ironically, her parents interpret as being for Tybalt's death.

Lord Capulet

There is extra dramatic tension in this scene because the audience knows that Romeo and Juliet are together in her room upstairs and several times there is raised the possibility that someone may go to speak to her. Out of consideration for her supposed grief, they decide not to disturb her.

Shakespeare's use of speed and haste in the play

This time it is Capulet's actions which bring the tragedy nearer, but again the cause is haste, speed and suddenness. The speed with which events happen in the play is emphasised again. It is now Monday night and the play's action began on Sunday morning, so that a period of only forty-eight hours has been covered. In this time there has been a brawl; Romeo has been in love with Rosaline; Paris has asked to marry Juliet and she has said she will consider it; a banquet has been held; Romeo has gone hoping to see Rosaline but has instead seen Juliet; Romeo and Juliet have fallen in love and he has spent the night talking to her in her garden; they have arranged to marry; Friar Laurence has agreed to perform the ceremony and has done so; there has been a second brawl; Tybalt has killed Mercutio; Romeo has killed Tybalt; Romeo has been banished but the Friar has promised to find a way to sort everything out.

Time

Act 3 Scene 5

Romeo and Juliet say farewell. Juliet refuses to marry Paris and her parents become angry. She decides to ask Friar Lawrence for help.

Romeo and Juliet have spent their wedding night together in her room. Juliet says that Romeo need not go yet because morning is a long way off. The night is their friend because it allows them to be together. So far in the play the light of day has been associated with different kinds of hot passion: lust, fighting and anger. Romeo says that as more and more light appears their sadness grows greater and greater.

Juliet

Romeo

Juliet says the birdsong they can hear is a nightingale and not a lark because she wants him to stay, but Romeo says that morning is here and it is indeed a lark. The animal imagery is used to underline their feelings. Juliet does not want the light in the sky to be that of daybreak because Romeo will have to leave for exile in Mantua. Romeo says that he will agree that it is not day if Juliet wishes, but that this would mean his death if he were to stay and be discovered. Romeo says he is prepared to die for love and the audience will know how ominous and ironic these words really are.

Juliet has a vision of Romeo dead in the tomb

Juliet says she has 'an ill-divining soul' and imagines that she sees Romeo dead

Juliet

in the bottom of a tomb. Both of them are pale, and Romeo says that 'sorrow drinks our blood', meaning that they look pale because they are sad. These are the last words Juliet ever hears from Romeo. This development of the imagery of drinking, where the body itself is now being consumed, joins later with the image of death coming to 'consume' Juliet in the tomb.

Key scene

Act 3, Scene 5 offers striking dramatic contrasts. Effectively it consists of four duologues, each one driving Juliet further back on her own resources. Her parting from Romeo is followed by three confrontations on the subject of her other 'marriage': the first cold, the second furious, the third disloyal and amoral.

Juliet's mother threatens to have Romeo poisoned

Lady Capulet

Lady Capulet demonstrates her callousness towards Juliet by censuring her supposed grief for Tybalt. She says that showing too much grief is foolish and that it would be better if Juliet were to weep because his murderer Romeo was still alive. The audience knows more than she does, so much of what Juliet says here to her mother will have a different meaning for them. See how many phrases you can find which have a different meaning for Juliet and for Lady Capulet. The audience, knowing the truth, can share in Juliet's deliberate deception of her mother. Notice how calm and mature Juliet is in facing her mother and how much she has changed from the girl we met at the start of the play.

Capulet flies into a fury at Juliet

Capulet arrives and his speech is full of ironic references to storms – ironic because it is he who will storm about in a short while when he hears that Juliet

Lord Capulet

Disorder

refuses to marry Paris. Notice how cruel Lady Capulet's remark is, and how ominous: 'I would the fool were married to her grave'. This very quickly comes tragically true and is another instance of the image of death as Juliet's suitor coming to claim her. Capulet flies into a terrible rage at Juliet and tells her she she is a traitor and will marry Paris even if he has to drag her to church on a 'hurdle' (a wooden frame used to draw traitors through the streets to their execution). Even Lady Capulet says that her husband is going too far, but he will not be pacified. Capulet says Juliet will never look him in the face again if she disobeys him and says that his 'fingers itch' (to strike her). He tells her she may beg and starve in the streets before he will have her disobey him. Capulet behaves tyrannically and refuses to listen to anyone else. Do you think we are intended to take the words of Juliet's parents absolutely literally? The stage producer (or the student) has to decide whether they are unnaturally cruel or whether grief, anxiety and fury are making them say things they do not really mean. There is no clear-cut answer to the question, but your opinion should take into account their behaviour elsewhere. You should also reflect that nearly all the characters talk of violence and death more freely than we would.

The Nurse tries to defend Juliet

Even though she is a trusted member of the household, the Nurse is abused

The Nurse

by Capulet when she tries to support Juliet. Juliet's parents cannot understand why she does not want to marry a rich husband. This was clearly Lady Capulet's attitude when she married Capulet. Juliet says that unless the marriage can at least be delayed, her bridal bed will be 'in that dim monument where Tybalt lies'. Her mother rejects her: she has 'done with' Juliet. In desperation Juliet turns to her Nurse.

Love

This scene is probably the best illustration of the failings of parental love in the play; even the Nurse, who has offered the equivalent of parental love, lets her down. Juliet's devotion to Romeo is thus the more striking, as is her independence: 'Thou [the nurse] and my bosom henceforth shall be twain.'

The Nurse fails Juliet's trust

The advice that the Nurse gives is that Juliet should make the best of things, keep quiet about her marriage to Romeo and marry Paris. The advice is well-intentioned and the Nurse seems to be trying to comfort and please her

The Nurse

Juliet

mistress, but Juliet is quietly furious and calls her a 'wicked fiend' when she has gone. This marks the severing of Juliet's esteem and friendship for her Nurse. Both Romeo and Juliet are now left almost completely alone, Romeo banished to Mantua and Juliet deserted by those to whom she looked for help and support. Only the Friar remains faithful and even he will fail them at their hour of greatest need in the tomb. Juliet now says that she will try the Friar's plan but, if it fails, she knows she has one final course of action left to her: 'If all else fail, myself have power to die.' Here the coming tragedy is signalled once again.

■ Self-test questions Act Three

Uncover the plot

Delete two of the three alternatives given, to find the correct plot. Beware possible misconceptions and muddles.

Tybalt, looking to fight Mercutio/Romeo/Benvolio, instead kills Mercutio/Benvolio/Paris, when the Prince/Benvolio/Romeo tries to intervene, but is then killed by an enraged Capulet/Benvolio/Romeo, who is sentenced to death/a fine/banishment. Juliet, distraught, sheds tears over Tybalt's wounds/Romeo's banishment/Tybalt's death. Romeo is told of his fate by Benvolio/the Duke/Friar Lawrence: they are joined by Juliet/the Nurse/Benvolio and make plans for Romeo to escape to Verona/Venice/Mantua. Capulet and Paris plan the wedding for Monday/Wednesday/Thursday. Meanwhile Romeo and Juliet part at dawn, on hearing a nightingale/lark/mockingbird. Juliet is told of the wedding plan by Lady Capulet/Lord Capulet/the Nurse, and refuses: her father threatens to kill her/to poison Romeo/to disown her. Let down even by the Nurse/the Friar/Paris, Juliet is left only with the last resort of death.

Who? What? Why? How?

1 Who is a 'dove-feather'd raven! wolfish-ravening lamb' – and why?
2 Who is thanked for 'comfort' by Romeo, and who by Juliet – and what's the difference?
3 What is the 'word there was, worser than Tybalt's death' for Juliet?
4 What is Friar Lawrence's four-point plan for Romeo?
5 Why does Lady Capulet think Juliet is weeping?
6 Why does Juliet change her mind and agree that it is day?
7 Why does Romeo love Tybalt 'better than thou canst devise'?
8 Why does Friar Lawrence tell Romeo he should be happy?
9 How does Benvolio say Romeo tried to avoid a fight with Tybalt?
10 How do the lovers tell that dawn is approaching – and how do they try to deny the fact?

Who said that?

1 Who says: 'Mercy but murders, pardoning those that kill'?
2 Who says: 'Either withdraw unto some private place,/Or reason coldly of your grievances'?

3 Who says: 'O calm, dishonourable, vile submission' – and why?
4 Who says: 'I would the fool were married to her grave' – of whom and why?
5 Who says: 'Your first is dead, or 'twere as good he were/As living here and you no use of him'?

Open quotes
Find the line – and complete the phrase or sentence.
1 ' "Romeo is banished" – to speak that word…'
2 'Yet "banished"? Hang up philosophy…'
3 'Is there no pity sitting in the clouds…'
4 'O God, I have an ill-divining soul!…'
5 'More light and light it grows!…'

Looking forward to the end?
For each of the following quotes, what is being talked about in the present – and why might it sound ominous, if you know what happens later in the play?
1 'Be fickle, fortune;/For then I hope, thou wilt not keep him long/But send him back.'
2 'Methinks I see thee, now thou art below,/As one dead in the bottom of a tomb.'
3 '..a poison, I would so temper it,/That Romeo should…/Soon sleep in quiet.'

Till death do us part
In this Act where weddings and deaths collide, find four lines from the text (hint: two by Juliet, one about her, and one about Romeo) linking marriage and the grave.

Act 4 Scene 1

Juliet meets Paris at Friar Lawrence's cell. She is cool towards Paris, and he leaves. The Friar explains to Juliet his plan to enable Romeo and her to be together.

Paris explains to Friar Lawrence that Capulet wants the marriage to take place

Time

quickly because he is concerned that Juliet is mourning too much for Tybalt's death. There are several ironies here. Juliet is mourning for the banishment of Romeo, for her husband's killing of her cousin and for the death of Tybalt. She has far more cause to grieve than Capulet can possibly know. The suggestion that marriage to Paris will in some way lessen Juliet's grief is obviously another serious error and will instead worsen her situation.

'Venus smiles not in a house of tears'

Paris

Paris' reference to Venus – the Roman goddess of love – is more appropriate than he knows. As well as the obvious sense, 'house' has an astrological meaning. A 'house' is one of the twelve signs of the zodiac and this again points up the influence of the stars on the fate of the lovers. This is the only time Paris meets Juliet. Paris is correct and well-mannered, and Juliet is very self-possessed and cool towards him and is clearly not sorry to see him leave.

Love

Paris's behaviour is above reproach. He speaks affectionately and reassuringly, putting only moderate pressure on Juliet. You will notice, though, how short all the speeches are: is there a sense of 'making conversation'? One comparison with Romeo: his 'holy kiss' when he leaves her. Think of Act 1, Scene 5.

Juliet says she will do anything to avoid the marriage to Paris

Juliet is desperate and tells the Friar that if he cannot help her she will kill herself with her knife. He says that if she is really determined to be free of Paris so as to be with Romeo, she might find the courage to try his plan. Juliet's speech beginning 'O, bid me leap, rather than marry Paris', shows how far she is prepared to go. Her words are chilling in the way they predict the future: 'bid me go into a new-made grave, and hide me with a dead man in his shroud.' (Some editions have 'tomb' instead of 'shroud' here.) Again we have the image of death as Juliet's lover.

Juliet

The Friar says that Juliet must seem to die

Friar Lawrence tells Juliet that she must secretly take the potion he has made, which will make it look as though she is dead. She will then be put into the Capulets' family tomb. The Friar will send a letter to Romeo and tell him of the plan, so that he and the Friar can come and rescue Juliet when she wakes up. The Friar's actions in this play, particularly after the banishment of Romeo, are not what you would expect from a holy man, though in his defence it should be said that, but for bad luck, he would have helped Romeo and Juliet to an unexpected happiness. His response is practical rather than moral, despite his lengthy speeches of advice. Do you think that he is morally right in helping them to their unofficial wedding night and, now, in taking the lead in Juliet's drugging herself to deceive her parents? Is it perhaps strange that he has a vial of such a potent draught ready to hand? The Friar's plan will require great courage of Juliet, especially as she will have to take the potion whilst she is alone. This increases the audience's sympathy for Juliet. She has become a bold and courageous woman, for she agrees to the Friar's plan without hesitation.

The Friar

Act 4 Scene 2

Juliet tells her father she will marry Paris and he brings the date of the wedding forward.

The Capulet household is busy and teeming with servants as arrangements are made for the wedding. Capulet needs twenty 'cunning cooks'. He seems to have forgotten his earlier opinion that the family should not be seen to 'revel much' after the death of Tybalt. Capulet's amusing exchange with the servant forms an effective contrast after the atmosphere of fear and haste in the previous scene.

Lord Capulet

Juliet returns from Friar Lawrence knowing what she must do and she tells her father that she will obey him and marry Paris. Capulet is overjoyed and praises the Friar, saying that the 'whole city is much bound to him'. Capulet assumes that the Friar has persuaded Juliet to obey his wishes and marry Paris. Capulet's praise is ironic, given the Friar's real part in the events that follow. What Juliet could not have anticipated, however, was her father's next move. Capulet decides that the wedding will take place the next day, that is, Wednesday instead of Thursday. This ruins the Friar's plan to write to Romeo. There is no real reason for moving the marriage date in this way. It is as though fate is leaving nothing to chance, just as it seemed once again as though things were about to work out happily for Romeo and Juliet. Juliet feels she has no other option but to go ahead with the Friar's plan and she is perhaps not aware of the problems which moving the date has caused the Friar.

Time

Act 4 Scene 3

Juliet drinks the potion the Friar has given her.

Juliet continues to show great self-control here and although present, the Nurse says nothing. This is unusual because the Nurse is normally never silent. When the Nurse and Lady Capulet leave, Juliet speaks the soliloquy which takes up the rest of this scene.

Juliet's soliloquy

Juliet

The courage and isolation of Juliet are emphasised in this speech. Later on, Romeo will have the same doubts about the poison he buys from the apothecary as those which Juliet has here about the Friar's potion. These parallels in the action and echoes in the imagery become more frequent towards the end of the play.

The terror and bravery of Juliet

Juliet

Juliet is afraid of what could go wrong with the plan. Notice the mouth imagery again as she describes the vault as having a 'foul mouth' where 'no healthsome air breathes in'. She fears that even if the plan works and she awakens safely, she may go mad surrounded by the dead bones of her ancestors. She is afraid that the Friar may have given her poison so as to conceal his own dishonour in having married her and Romeo in secret.

Ironically, she worries about what might happen if she awakens early, but not about what might go wrong if she awakens too late, which is what actually happens. She has taken the precaution of bringing her knife with her in case the potion does not work at all; she clearly intends to carry out her threatened suicide if this is necessary.

Love

Juliet's courage is remarkable. Her entire soliloquy is full of genuine reasons not to take the potion: it may not work, Friar Lawrence may have decided to poison her, the fears of waking in the tomb. Such is her love for Romeo that all she needs against these objections is the thought of his (their) happiness: 'Romeo! Romeo! Romeo! I drink to thee.'

Juliet's haste to take the Friar's potion reveals her desperate state and re-emphasises the speed of dramatic action. All the older characters except the Friar have now rejected Juliet. He too lets her down by failing to get the letter through. The Friar is also tragically late arriving at the tomb. This last failing is particularly serious. He is very precise about how long the potion will work; he tells Juliet it will work for forty-two hours, so he of all people knows for how long the potion will take effect and when Juliet should therefore awaken.

Act 4 Scene 4

The Nurse goes to awaken Juliet.

This brief scene concentrates on the minor domestic problems of the Capulets,

Time

as they rush around making last-minute preparations for the wedding. The scene is a sharp contrast to the terror and stillness of the previous scene and also to the next one, when Juliet's body is discovered. Notice how the imagery of the mouth, of food, and of eating and drinking link the scenes together. Capulet makes much mention of time and the need to hurry: the second cock has crowed, the curfew bell has rung, it is three o'clock in the morning. This continual emphasis on speed underlines the feeling of inevitability and of events moving inexorably to their climax.

Lord Capulet

As dawn breaks for the fourth time in the play and the servants rush about, Capulet again cries for more and more haste and sends the Nurse to rouse Juliet for her wedding. Capulet's amiability is restored now that he thinks he is getting his own way.

It might be suggested that Capulet appears in his most favourable light arranging and organising domestic affairs: feasts, parties and so forth. You can no doubt find him bustling and bumbling in a cheerful welcoming haste on more than one occasion in the play. Does Lady Capulet also appear less cold at such times?

Act 4 Scene 5

Juliet is discovered apparently dead. The wedding becomes a wake.

Juliet

The Nurse is as usual full of chatter about the pleasures of the flesh. She says she hopes Juliet has had plenty of sleep because she will get little rest on her wedding night. This apparent relaxation of the mood actually serves to increase the tension in the play because of the audience's knowledge of what is to happen.

'Alas, alas! Help, help! My lady's dead!'

Nature

The Nurse calls for 'aqua vitae' (brandy, although ironically the words literally mean 'water of life'). Lady Capulet cries that unless Juliet wakes she will die with her. Compare this with Lady Montague's later reaction to Romeo's exile. Juliet's father arrives to see his daughter and says that death 'lies on her like an untimely frost'. His words about Juliet reintroduce the flower imagery and are ironic because Juliet's 'untimely' death is not really death at all. Notice how often Shakespeare makes use of irony in this play, even when the Friar arrives and asks if Juliet is ready to go to church and Capulet replies 'ready to go, but never to return'. This is of course a double irony, because Capulet does not know that the Friar already knows about what has happened and knows more about the truth than Capulet does.

Notice how Shakespeare does not allow the tragedy of this scene to overshadow the powerful impact of the tragic climax at the end of the play. Shakespeare holds down the tragedy here by keeping this scene short and by placing it between two other sections of lighter mood.

Capulet says that death has taken Juliet for his bride

Lord Capulet

Capulet tells Paris that death has claimed Juliet for his own, but does so in a way that echoes the sexual death-as-lover imagery in the play and connects it with the imagery of flowers by saying that death has 'deflowered' (taken the virginity of) Juliet.

You will notice that, after the news is broken to Paris, each of the four mourners has a formal speech, all of about the same length, expressing grief. Lady Capulet curses the day and the Nurse then picks up the same theme in a speech that veers towards the ludicrous, with its constant repetition of variations on 'O day!'. Both Paris and Capulet use similar exclamations ('O love! O life!' / 'O child! O child!') and echo

Love and passion

Lady Capulet in beginning with a whole line of distressing adjectives. We are not meant to doubt that each loves Juliet in his or her own way, but you should consider whether this use of a sort of formula for grief is somehow impersonal.

The Friar tells them all to accept heaven's will with good grace. He mentions the image of rosemary – a flower associated with remembrance and the dead – that the Nurse introduced earlier in the play as Juliet's favourite flower, although significantly she linked it then with Romeo.

A comic interlude ends this scene, with the musicians, who have come to play at the wedding, saying to the Nurse that they may as well pack up and be gone. This interlude with Peter may seem rather out of place after what has just happened, even though we know that Juliet is not really dead, but in the second half of the play virtually the only comic relief comes from the clownish servant characters. It would be thought too harrowing to move directly from Juliet's 'death' to Romeo's preparation for his. Dramatically, this little scene serves its purpose well, though you will probably find some inconsistency in Peter's behaviour. Oddly, the contrasting moods are summed up by the two meanings of 'dump': 'doleful dumps' are sorrows, but a dump is also a dance.

The Friar's speech is cleverly constructed to underline the unreality of Juliet's death, although what he says and what is understood by the other characters and by the audience will not be the same. Capulet's reply includes a list of opposites: 'wedding cheer to sad burial feast', 'solemn hymns to sullen dirges'. These take up a central theme of the play – the contrast between surface appearance and when 'all things change them to the contrary'.

■ Self-test questions Act Four

Uncover the plot
Delete two of the three alternatives given, to find the correct plot. Beware possible misconceptions and muddles.

Paris/the Nurse/Capulet is at Friar Lawrence's cell, informing him that the wedding is now to be on Wednesday/Thursday/Friday. Juliet comes to plead for help, saying she will poison herself/jump from a tower/stab herself rather than marry Paris. The Friar gives her a 'vial' or potion/liquor/bottle, containing a substance which will make her appear shrunk/dead/asleep for 42/36/24 hours, after which she will awake in the charnel house/graveyard/Capulet vault, to be met by Romeo/Paris/the Nurse. Juliet agrees to marry Paris, to the delight of her Nurse/father/mother, who advances the wedding again to Wednesday/Thursday/Monday. Alone, Juliet takes the potion, with a vial of poison/dagger/rapier by her side. The family mourn her 'death', restrained by the knowing figure of Capulet/Paris/Friar Lawrence.

Who? What? Why?

1 Who is supposed to find Juliet dead – and who does so?
2 What are the symptoms of the Friar's potion?
3 What reason does Paris give the Friar for the wedding's being brought forward?
4 What does the Friar tell Juliet to do first of all?
5 What does 'the manner of our country' dictate will happen to Juliet when she is found 'dead'?
6 What is Romeo's part in the plan supposed to be ?
7 What does Juliet worry about, before taking the potion?
8 Why is Friar Lawrence confident that Juliet will go along with his plan?
9 Why is the 'death' scene not wholly tragic, and why might Shakespeare have done this?
10 Why does the Nurse say Juliet should 'sleep for a week'?

Who said that?

1 Who says: 'Venus smiles not in a house of tears?
2 Who says: 'My dismal scene I needs must act alone'?
3 Who says: 'Revive, look up, or I will die with thee!'?
4 Who says: 'And weep ye now, seeing she is advanc'd/Above the clouds, as high as heaven itself'?
5 Who says: 'Ay, let the County take you in your bed'?

About time

1 How do we know what time of day it is when Capulet sends for Juliet to be wakened?
2 How do we know that the wedding has been brought forward to Wednesday?
3 How do we know that even Lady Capulet thinks the wedding is rather rushed?
4 How many times does Capulet say, 'Make haste' in Act 4 Sc 4?
5 How do we know that Capulet feels the untimeliness of Juliet's death very keenly?

Looking forward to the end?

Why does each of the following sound ominous, if you know what happens later in the play?
1 Juliet vows to kill herself with her dagger, if the Friar cannot help her.
2 Juliet worries about waking up too early in the vault – or going mad and killing herself.
3 Capulet cries 'Death is my son-in-law, Death is my heir.'

The seeds of truth?

What is the contribution of the following plant images to the meaning of the events being discussed?
1 'an untimely frost/Upon the sweetest flower of all the field'
2 'green in earth'
3 'like mandrakes torn out of the earth.'
4 'Stick your rosemary on this fair corse'
5 'Our bridal flowers serve for a burial corse'
6 'The roses in thy lips and cheeks shall fade'

Act 5 Scene 1

Romeo is in exile in Mantua and receives a message that Juliet is dead. He buys poison and plans to return to Verona to join Juliet in death.

Romeo

As his servant arrives in Mantua from Verona, Romeo talks of a prophetic dream he has had where Juliet found him dead. Balthasar has rushed to tell Romeo that he has seen Juliet laid to rest in the Capulet tomb, not knowing the truth. Romeo vows to go to Verona, saying that he will defy the stars, meaning that he defies fate to do any worse to him. It is Romeo's haste at this point that makes the tragedy certain, ignoring Balthasar's counsel to be patient and thus arriving too early for the Friar to intercept him at the tomb.

Romeo says he will lie with Juliet in the tomb

Disorder

In his soliloquy, Romeo echoes the imagery of Death lying with Juliet, with its sexual as well as literal meaning: 'Well, Juliet, I will lie with thee tonight' but the ominous meaning is that he will join her in death. Notice that, appropriately, 'lie' can also mean falsehood and we know that Juliet is not really dead.

Love

Death and love are frequent companions in the words and thoughts of Romeo and Juliet, yet we do not think of them as morbid. Life is so intertwined with love that the loss of the lover is equivalent to death.

The shop of the apothecary

Nature

The description of the apothecary is very corpse-like as though he is another image of death in the play, which in a way he is. The apothecary's shop is described as being full of ugly reptiles and fish and dried-up remnants of living things. The boxes are empty, the seeds 'musty', the cakes of roses old and scattered. Juliet's image of 'green earth' appears again with its connection with 'festering'. The apothecary is equivalent to the Friar in his knowledge of plants, herbs and the laws of nature. The apothecary's skill is an illustration of what the Friar spoke of in his first speech, just before Romeo entered: 'Virtue itself turns vice being misapplied'.

Romeo buys poison

Romeo says that the apothecary is 'so full of wretchedness' that he should not fear to break the law and risk the death penalty. Look very carefully at Romeo's description of the apothecary and you will see that he is in many

51

Romeo

ways describing himself: 'the world is not thy friend, nor the world's law'. Romeo's contempt for the gold that he uses to pay for the poison – 'worse poison to men's souls' – is an ironic comment on the attitude of Juliet's parents to true love; 'the great rich Capulet' and his callous wife who think, like the Nurse, that marriage is merely to do with physical passion or a commercial transaction. 'I sell thee poison, thou hast sold me none' he says to the apothecary, and gives him forty gold coins (ducats). This scene is another important turning-point in the action of the play and you will see many similarities between it and the marriage scene in the Friar's cell; notice the parallels of tone and imagery.

Act 5 Scene 2

Friar Lawrence's message has failed to get to Romeo.

Time

The Friar

Bad luck strikes again as Friar John tells Friar Lawrence that he was delayed getting out of the city to deliver the message to Romeo because an outbreak of plague prevented him leaving an infected house. He returns the Friar's letter to Romeo undelivered.

The action again speeds up after the last quiet scene as Friar Lawrence is thrown into despair by this news. Juliet is due to awaken within three hours. Friar Lawrence will go and get her from the tomb and hide her in his cell until another message can be sent to Romeo. Friar Lawrence has always had a calm solution to each situation. The build-up of tension is therefore increased when we find him in haste, talking of danger and sending for a crow-bar. Once again, though, the ingenious Friar has a solution, explained in his brief soliloquy. This time the audience knows that his solution will not work: why?

Act 5 Scene 3

Romeo arrives at the tomb, meets Paris there and kills him. Believing Juliet to be dead, Romeo takes the poison and dies. Juliet awakens, sees Romeo dead and commits suicide. Capulet and Montague promise never to feud again.

Romeo

Paris has come at night to Juliet's tomb to visit his 'sweet flower', put flowers on her grave and pay his respects. Although he seems rather formal and sentimental in his speech, he is genuinely sincere in the same way that Romeo was sincere in his love-sickness for Rosaline. His comment on hearing his servant's warning whistle is ironic: 'what cursed foot wanders this way tonight', because we know it is Romeo. This whole scene is filled with ironic parallels. Paris anticipates events by thinking that Juliet has died of grief for Tybalt, when she is soon to die of grief for Romeo. Just as Romeo hid in the darkness and overheard Juliet first speak of her love for him, so here Paris hides in the darkness and overhears Romeo at her tomb. Paris, the rival lover, brings flowers to the tomb of Juliet and meets the other 'rival lover' in the play, death, in the form of Romeo.

The imagery of the mouth

Romeo arrives to 'descend into this bed of death', giving his servant the excuse

Disorder

that he wants a precious ring from Juliet's finger. He warns his servant that if he returns to see what else Romeo intends to do he will 'tear thee joint by joint and strew this hungry churchyard with thy limbs'. He says that he is 'savage-wild', 'fierce', 'inexorable' as wild animals 'or the roaring sea'. The images of 'hungry' death and 'inexorable' fate appear throughout this scene.

The body and food are associated in their most clear form with the mouth imagery of death as Romeo descends into the 'womb of death' through its 'detestable maw' that has gorged itself on Juliet, 'the dearest morsel of the earth'. He forces open the tomb's 'rotten jaws' and says he will cram it with 'more food', meaning his own corpse.

Can vengeance be pursued further than death?

Romeo

Paris thinks that Romeo has come to pursue the family feud by revenging himself on Juliet's dead body and he asks one of the play's central questions when he says 'can vengeance be pursu'd further than death?' Paris interrupts Romeo and with unconscious irony tells him 'thou must die'.

Characters

The death of Paris offers hints at more devotion than he shows elsewhere in the play. He has come to the tomb at night (admittedly speaking formal verse about a conventional act, strewing flowers). He challenges one who, he thinks, is desecrating the tomb. We still cannot see Paris as a passionate figure, but Romeo's rival is worthy, unselfish and honourable.

Romeo

Romeo's sad reply is an echo of his reply to Tybalt's invitation to fight with him, when he tells Paris 'I love thee better than myself'. Paris' servant sees them fighting and runs for help, but Paris is killed. This fatal confrontation marks the only time in the play when Paris and Romeo actually meet.

The imagery of light

Romeo says he will bury Paris with Juliet but that it will not be in a grave

Light and darkness

but in 'a lantern', because Juliet's beauty makes the tomb 'full of light'. Again the beauty of Juliet is compared by Romeo to brilliant light, even in death, and his speech is full of wordplay on 'lightning', which should remind you of Juliet's worry that their love resembled lightning too much. The lovers' passion has been described by the imagery as almost religious and heavenly, and the Friar warned that too much passion was dangerous and would consume itself 'like fire and powder'.

Romeo's final soliloquy

Romeo's long and final speech in the play is a beautiful soliloquy in which

Romeo

Light and darkness

death is spoken of as sucking 'the honey' of Juliet's breath and ironically Romeo, thinking that Juliet is beautiful even in death, remarks that it has 'no power' over her beauty and her lips and cheeks are still crimson. He does not know that the colour is returning to her lips and cheeks because she is about to awaken and thinks instead that 'Death is amorous' and keeps her ever-beautiful in the tomb to be his lover. The play's images of the dawn and fire and light symbolising the beauty that chases away the darkness of night have finally met in this last mysterious irony; here at the final dawn in the play, Juliet is Life in Death. Romeo drinks the poison and dies, and within a few lines Juliet is awake and asking for him by name. Romeo has been destroyed by fate and his impetuous haste has been his final undoing. The imagery of drinking has come full circle from its start in the joy of life at Capulet's feast to this point of death and tragedy.

Juliet awakens and is left alone for the last time

The Friar

Juliet

The Friar arrives but is too late to save the lives of Paris or Romeo. He urges the awakened Juliet to escape with him and underlines the role of fate in the play when he tells her that 'a greater power than we can contradict hath thwarted our intents'. Unable to persuade her to leave, the Friar panics and runs away.

The last reference to drinking in the play occurs when Juliet cannot find a 'friendly drop' of poison in the cup in Romeo's hand. She kills herself with the dagger in order to be with her husband in death. Juliet's suicide is the traditional death of the noble warrior who is defeated but will not be enslaved. This is a fitting end for someone who has been throughout the stronger and more practical of the lovers and who has had to face danger alone.

Servants and watchmen appear, discover the bodies of Paris, Romeo and Juliet, and arrest Romeo's servant Balthasar and Friar Lawrence pending Prince Escalus's arrival. Lord and Lady Capulet enter, followed by the Prince. Montague arrives with the news that his wife has died of grief over Romeo's exile.

Love

The last scene ends in the triumph of love over hate. The love of Romeo and Juliet gains a fitting memorial, but what of parental love? The deaths of the lovers kill one mother and nearly kill the other: where has this devotion been previously? Interestingly, though their remarks are full of love, grief and guilt, the parents are given very little to say.

The healing power of love

Love **and passion**

Love has proved stronger than hatred, stronger even than death, but the play is almost as much about hatred as about love. It seems to be an important message of the play that love is even stronger than the power of fate. Love has taught society a lesson. The audience knew from the start of the play that Romeo and Juliet would die, but their death holds hope for the future. Love has changed the world of Verona.

Who was most to blame?

Disorder

Do you feel that at the end of the play the Capulets and Montagues have been equally punished by fate for their feud? See if you can establish which of the families was more to blame for events. The Prince points out that he, too, has lost 'a brace of kinsmen' (Mercutio and Paris) and seems to accept some blame for what has happened. How far do you think he is responsible for the tragedy?

Order is finally restored

In order to defend himself from suspicion, Friar Lawrence makes a long chorus-like speech near the end of the play in which he reviews what has happened. This dramatic device enables Shakespeare to ensure that the audience understands and remembers the plot of the play and, by allowing Balthasar to complete the story, introduces the letter from Romeo to support

Lord Capulet

the Friar's account and to reveal the events in Mantua.

Appropriately, it is the fiery-tempered Capulet who asks for Montague's hand in peace. The feuding families agree to live in peace and say they will put up golden statues to Romeo and Juliet. This last reference is unintentionally ironic because the audience will recall what Romeo told the apothecary about gold and what it represents in the world.

Light and darkness

The appearance of the Prince at the very end of the play emphasises the political point of the play: that society depends upon order and obedience to authority. The Prince proclaims these things on each of his three appearances. The imagery of light is used finally by the Prince when he says that on this last day 'the sun for sorrow will not show his head', finally underlining the darkness (in many senses) in which the play closes and the way heaven is in sympathy with the dead lovers.

Of all the six characters who die in the play, only the loving Lady Montague is not young. This underlines how the play concentrates on the passionate world of the young and the way in which it is they who must pay the price for the mischievous and quarrelsome folly of the old.

■ Self-test questions Act Five

Uncover the plot
Delete two of the three alternatives given, to find the correct plot. Beware possible misconceptions and muddles.

Benvolio/Friar John/Balthasar arrives in Verona/Mantua/Venice with news of Juliet's early marriage/escape plan/death. Romeo seeks out a Franciscan Friar/ beggar/apothecary to buy a cordial/poison/dagger. Meanwhile, Friar Lawrence learns that his messenger Friar John/Balthasar/Friar Francis has not got through. Capulet/Paris/Montague is at the vault when Romeo arrives, tries to arrest/kill/fight him, and is killed. Wondering that Juliet looks so pale/merry/fair, Romeo poisons himself. Friar Lawrence/Balthasar/the Page arrives too late. Juliet, finding Romeo dead, kills herself with the dregs of the poison/the poison on his lips/his dagger. Montague and Capulet are reconciled, with the pledge of a 'glooming peace'/ a 'jointure'/a 'statue in pure gold' as a final tribute to the lovers.

Who? What? Where? When? Why?
1 Who is asked to account for events, following the discovery of the bodies in the vault?
2 Who is the first to ask for his former enemy's hand in peace?
3 What has happened to Lady Montague?
4 What dream has Romeo had in Mantua – and why is it ironic?
5 What is Friar Lawrence's emergency plan, when he realises the first has failed?
6 Where was Friar John delayed, and why?
7 Why does Romeo choose the particular apothecary that he does?
8 How long before Juliet is due to awake does Friar Lawrence meet Friar John? How long before her awakening does he arrive at the vault?
9 Why does Friar Lawrence flee?
10 Why does Paris think Juliet died?

Who said that?
1 Who says: 'If I may trust the flattering truth of sleep/My dreams presage some joyful news at hand' – and why is this ironic?

2 Who says: 'Thou detestable maw, thou womb of death/Gorg'd with the dearest morsel of the earth'?

3 Who says: 'Can vengeance be pursued further than death?' – and why, and what more does this say to the audience of the play?

4 Who says: 'And I, for winking at your discords too,/Have lost a brace of kinsmen'?

Open quotes

Find the line – and complete the phrase or sentence.

1 'A greater power than we can contradict...'
2 'There is thy gold – ...'
3 'Death, that hath suck'd the honey of thy breath...'
4 'See what a scourge is laid upon your hate...'

Parallel lines

The final scene is full of echoes. Where else do you hear something like the following lines?

1 'Here's to my love' (as Romeo drinks poison)
2 '(She) breathed such life with kisses in my lips/That I reviv'd' (Romeo's dream)
3 'I descend into this bed of death' (Romeo entering the vault)
4 'Shake the yoke of inauspicious stars/From this world-wearied flesh.' (Romeo resolving to die)
5 'Thou desperate pilot, now at once run on/The dashing rocks thy sea-sick weary bark.' (Romeo about to drink poison)

■ How to write a coursework essay

Most of you will use your study of *Romeo and Juliet* to write a coursework essay fulfilling the Shakespeare requirement for English and English Literature. In writing this essay, you must meet certain requirements. In particular, you must show awareness (though not necessarily at great length) of social and historical influences, cultural contexts and literary traditions. These can be covered in various ways. The literary traditions of the use of a Chorus and the inevitability of tragedy are relevant, for instance, as is the tradition of using the sonnet as an expression of love. This could also be seen as a social and cultural comment on Elizabethan society. Historically, the presentation of a city state divided by feuds between great families is a vivid presentation of Renaissance Italy. Details from the form of the duel to the normal age of marriage, as well as larger issues like the role of parents, also provide social, historical and cultural material.

It is also essential that you show considerable evidence of textual knowledge, even if the essay has a strong creative element. Types of response might include:

- scene analysis;
- character study;
- analysis of imagery and other linguistic features;
- dramatic effect of the play or one or more scenes;
- empathic response to character;
- reflections on a production.

If you are writing an analytical essay, the *most important consideration* is that you must develop an argument or explain a point of view throughout. There is little to be gained by listing the meetings between Romeo and Juliet. What is important is that you relate these meetings to your theme: the characters of the lovers compared, the way their love is presented in the play, the contrast between their love and other so-called loves, or whatever you are writing about. Careful advance preparation will aid you in organising your theme or argument: making notes on the material, putting these notes in order, then working through two or three drafts of the essay. By doing this you can reach a decision on what each paragraph is to be about, as far as possible signalling this to the reader in the opening sentence, often called a *topic sentence* because it introduces the topic of the paragraph.

If you choose an imaginative/creative essay, the *first essential* is to reveal throughout your factual knowledge of the text and a soundly based interpretation of it. Mere imagination will not gain credit in textual study for GCSE English Literature.

The length of your essay will depend on the type of essay you write, your own wishes and your teacher's advice, but do bear in mind that it is only one of several pieces of coursework: there is no need for a 5000 word blockbuster.

Love

Examine how Shakespeare presents love in a variety of forms in Romeo and Juliet. *Consider how different characters interpret the meaning and importance of love.*

This is an essay where the main problem is organising huge blocks of material: there is no problem finding the material!

The longest section will obviously be about Romeo and Juliet. It is probably advisable to start with that, though you could do the opposite and build up to it at the end of the essay. If you start with Romeo and Juliet, make sure that your introduction explains something of the structure of the essay, so that the reader does not think that you are concentrating on them alone.

It is impossible to deal with all there is to write about the love of Romeo and Juliet: instead, here are a few reminders of some important points. Their love transforms them; compare before and after in each case. Their scenes together are treated in the most romantic way: the sonnet at first meeting while the world stands still, the setting of orchard and balcony, etc. Their love gives them other noble qualities of maturity, devotion, courage, independence, etc. The connection with death that is ever-present shows that their lives only exist together. Their love finally has the power to overcome hatred, though they are destroyed by it (and fate/chance). Each of these points is worth at least a long paragraph and you also need to describe (with copious reference and quotation) the details of their relationship.

Shakespeare provides every sort of contrast to the luminous central relationship. You could perhaps deal with conventional love next. Paris is always correct and no doubt affectionate, but there is no hint of passion; he is a respectable and rich young man and he obeys Juliet's father. The Romeo/Rosaline affair is similar in its lack of depth, but more self-indulgently melancholy: perhaps it is as well we never see Rosaline as Romeo's feelings are directed more at himself than the supposed target of his affections.

Some people dismiss love: Mercutio by his words; Tybalt by his actions. There is an anti-romantic culture among the young of Verona.

There are, of course, other kinds of love than sexual or romantic. This play is about families, but parental love is in short supply. These people love their children, their final grief shows that, but they have other priorities and neglect their children, or worse. The Montagues' family life is simply omitted, but the Capulets show little love as parents and also have a false idea of love for Juliet: making a conventionally successful marriage is what matters to them.

There are characters who partially take the place of parental love (the Nurse and the Friar), but who ultimately fail Romeo and Juliet. You might even suggest that both are in error in trying to keep Romeo and Juliet happy without thinking enough about what is right. Juliet is terrifyingly committed to what is right in a way that shames the older people. As a representative of Christian love, Friar Lawrence tries hard, but never solves the conflict between Christian teaching and worldly desires.

As a conclusion you might find as many examples as you can of the way in which the love of Romeo and Juliet rises above the actions of the other characters. For instance, the selflessness of the lovers contrasts with the selfishness of most other characters: even Friar Lawrence tries to run away from the tomb. Surprisingly, and interestingly, there are two other possible examples of self-sacrifice. Mercutio is so enraged by Romeo's meek behaviour to Tybalt that he feels the need to redeem his friend's honour, the cynic in love proving more dedicated in friendship. Paris, in the final scene, paying homage to Juliet and opposing the supposed grave-robber, hints at greater devotion than Shakespeare has previously chosen to reveal.

Characters

Clearly the two characters about whom there is most to write are Romeo and Juliet. However, we have already commented on them at length in the **Love** essay. Therefore, let us examine a different set of people for this essay.

In depicting Veronese society Shakespeare creates a contrasting set of young noblemen. Examine the characters of Mercutio, Benvolio, Paris and Tybalt; compare and contrast them and explain their roles in the play.

The first striking similarity between the characters is how comparatively few scenes each appears in. Three of them belong only to the first half of the play (up to Act 3, Scene 1) and the fourth, Paris, belongs largely to the second half: by the time Mercutio and Tybalt are breathing their last, he has spoken a mere four lines.

This suggests that these characters are created by Shakespeare more for their roles than their characters. In other words, their importance is in the part they play in the plot or in the main characters' relationships rather than their individuality. This is certainly true of Benvolio and Paris, true to some extent of Tybalt and untrue of Mercutio.

As characters, Benvolio and Paris are defined by their roles and it might be a good idea to deal with them simply and clearly at the start. Benvolio is the good and sensible friend, Paris the conventionally worthy lover. Each is thus a contrast to Romeo. Benvolio spends the first half of the play as the level-headed one in a trio of friends that includes a love-sick melancholic and a bawdy cynic with an out-of-control sense of humour. His character is convincing enough, but he does seem always to be the one explaining Romeo's latest exploits, from dawn walks to fatal combat. When Romeo is banished, there is no further use for Benvolio. There is, then, much more use for Paris, the socially desirable alternative to Romeo. Paris offers contrast, but also has a crucial plot involvement as Juliet's husband-to-be. Presented sympathetically (as in his death), Paris can hardly be seen as an in-depth character.

Tybalt's personality is much stronger, but he remains two-dimensional. His role is to represent the violence underlying the lovers' relationship and to provide, by his death, the fatal step towards tragedy. Tybalt does one thing in the play and keeps on doing it: he fights Montagues, or he tries to fight Montagues, or he sends messages challenging Montagues. Typically, we never see the good qualities Juliet and the Nurse speak of.

Mercutio's character has more individuality and his role is less clear-cut. His role as Romeo's companion could be filled by a less striking individual and, though his death is a crucial stage in the play, the same effect in terms of plot could have been achieved by Romeo simply killing Tybalt. Mercutio's cynicism, wit, bawdy language, flouting of convention and, ultimately, loyalty to his friend make him a complex character. It is interesting that he is the only one of the four whose character is subject to different opinions and interpretations: on stage you know what the other three will be like, but Mercutio can be a stylish dandy with rapier-like wit, or a foul-mouthed boor plagued by a profound dislike for other people and himself.

Given the nature of the young men, you will probably consider character and role together, but there is another aspect of their roles that you should deal with more briefly. As a group they sum up attitudes in Verona: in a city torn by feuding between great families, what better summary of social attitudes than the behaviour of young noblemen? You can identify the whole range of responses to life in the city from the murderous to the responsible. All are affected by the feud: even Paris, who seems outside the conflict, dies violently as an indirect result of it.

You are asked to compare and contrast these characters. Contrasting them individually is straightforward: we have already considered suitable comments. Another form of contrast is between and within families. Six young nobles are important characters in the play: Juliet and five men. An interesting comparison is to show that violence and good sense do not belong to any one family. Each pair of cousins is strongly contrasted: Juliet and Tybalt (Capulet), Romeo and Benvolio (Montague), Paris and Mercutio (Royal Family).

You can conclude by summarising your arguments: this is perfectly acceptable. As a variant, you could examine another reason for the number of young men in the play. Juliet is presented within her family. Romeo is never seen at home and is presented with his own generation. Mercutio, Benvolio and Tybalt (not Paris), plus the Friar, are the dramatic equivalent of Juliet's family and Nurse.

Empathic approach to character: it is also possible to write a more imaginative piece by examining the play as one of the characters, reflecting his/her opinions and personality. The Nurse and the Friar would be excellent choices for an empathic essay: they are involved in the action, they are crucial to many of the plots, but they are still able to observe the principals. Their opinions and moral positions are obvious, and the lovers confide in them.

Key scene

It is important to remember that *Romeo and Juliet* really belongs on the stage, not in the classroom, and it is possible to write about it in this way. You can concentrate on one scene or comment on one or more productions.

Examine the dramatic effectiveness and significance to the play of Act 3, Scene 1 or Act 3, Scene 5 of Romeo and Juliet.

There are many other scenes you could choose: Act 2, Scene 2 and Act 5, Scene 3 would both be good choices. However, we are going to examine how you could approach one of the two key scenes in Act 3.

You need to examine how the scene itself has dramatic impact. If you can write from the experience of seeing a stage production, so much the better. In the case of Scene 1 you will write about the tension, the violence and the sheer excitement of the action. Scene 5 contains intense love poetry, vivid contrasts, violent verbal conflict and an acute sense of the growing isolation of Juliet.

You will wish to examine what we learn of the characters from the scene you have chosen. Tybalt and Mercutio are revealed with great dramatic force and Romeo is presented as the victim of a tragic dilemma in Scene 1, as indeed is Juliet in the later scene. The characters (and failings) of parents and nurse are brought out well as they desert Juliet.

It is important to show how the scene fits into the overall dramatic pattern. In different ways both these scenes are watersheds, climaxing the developments of the first half of the play, dictating the pattern for the second half. The ever-present feud claims three victims in Scene 1 (two dead, Romeo banished) and establishes that the second half will be the potentially tragic story of a secret and separated marriage. Scene 5 completes the love story in one sense (the marriage night/last meeting) and also tells the story of Romeo's exile from Verona and makes clear that in future Juliet will not be able to reach any kind of compromise with her family. Her story is now one of risks taken with the Friar's guidance.

Placing either of these scenes as a crucial part of the play is not difficult and should be done at some length. However, you might also like to examine the way these scenes reflect others in the play. Act 3, Scene 1, is a more tragic re-run of Act 1, Scene 1: how are the scenes similar; in what ways do they differ? Act 3, Scene 5, has echoes of many scenes: the Balcony Scenes and two others (Act 2, Scene 5/Act 3, Scene 2) that begin with Juliet alone and in which the Nurse brings news of how her love is progressing. Here she is with Romeo, of course, and the Nurse is joined by her parents, but the pattern is similar.

You should consider also how you think this scene should be staged or how you have seen it staged, or both. Comments on scenery and costumes are perfectly acceptable, but are not the only points to be made. How do the characters relate to each? How does stage position help this? How are crucial key speeches delivered?

Commentary on production: In the case of *Romeo and Juliet* you have the opportunity to compare a modern film that altered the setting of the play, with a production you may have seen on stage, or a traditional production on television. This could be a good choice, but remember not to concentrate simply on externals. Think about what is gained and lost by the setting, the interpretation of the characters, the creation of mood and atmosphere, the emphasis on one scene or another, etc.

■ How to write an examination essay

Most of you will study *Romeo and Juliet* as a coursework text, but it is useful to consider the approach to an examination essay on the play. The advice given below will be useful in helping you to approach any English Literature examination essays.

Before you start writing

- The first essential is thorough revision. It is important that you realise that even Open Book examinations require close textual knowledge. You will have time to look up quotations and references, *but only if you know where to look*.

- Read the questions very carefully, both to choose the best one and to take note of *exactly what you are asked to do*. Questions in an examination are likely to be on subjects similar to those considered in **How to write a coursework essay**, but you must make sure you know what is being asked: an astonishing number of candidates answer the question they *imagine or hope* has been asked. If you are asked to consider different types of love in the play, for instance, do not confine yourself to Romeo and Juliet. Their love may be the most important part of the essay, but you are also required to examine Romeo/Rosaline and Juliet/Paris, plus parental love, friendship, etc.

- Identify all the key words in the question that mention characters, events and themes, and instructions as to what to do: e.g. compare, contrast, comment, give an account, etc. Write a short list of the things you have to do.

- Look at each of the points you have identified and jot down what you are going to say about each.

- Decide in what order you are going to deal with the question's main points. Number them in sequence. Do not adopt a chronological approach unless you have a specific reason for doing so.

Writing the essay

- The first sentences are important. Try to summarise your approach to the question so the examiner has some idea of how you plan to approach it. Do not begin, 'Romeo meets Juliet at a ball which he gate-crashes after meeting the servant who has the invitations.' A suitable opening for an essay on types of love might be, 'The love between Romeo and Juliet dominates the play. However, we are able to appreciate its intensity and self-sacrifice even more because of a background that emphasises superficial forms of love as well as passionate hatred.' Jump straight into the essay, do not nibble at its extremities for a page and a half. A personal response will be rewarded, but you must always answer the question: as you write the essay *refer back to your list of points*.

- Answer *all the question*. Many students spend all their time answering just one part of a question and ignoring the rest. This prevents you gaining marks for the parts left out. In the same way, failing to answer enough questions on the examination is a waste of marks that can always be gained most easily at the start of an answer.

- There is no 'correct' length for an essay. What you must do is spend the full time usefully in answering all parts of the question (spending longer than the allocated time by more than a few minutes is dangerous). Some people write faster than others: they don't always get the best marks!

- Take care with presentation, spelling and punctuation. It is generally unwise to use slang or contractions (e.g. 'they've' for 'they have').

- Use quotation or paraphrase when it is relevant and contributes to the quality and clarity of your answer. References to events often do not need quotation, but it is impossible to bring out, for instance, the use of imagery to convey Romeo and Juliet's love without using the exact words. In any case, *extended* quotations are usually unhelpful, and padding is a waste of time.

■ Self-test answers Act One

Uncover the plot

In Verona, a fight between Montagues and Capulets is broken up by the Prince. Romeo tells Benvolio the cause of his sadness: his love for Rosaline. Meanwhile, Paris asks Capulet for Juliet's hand. A Capulet servant, with supper invitations, seeks Romeo's help to read the list: Romeo decides to go to the feast for 'the fair Rosaline'. Lady Capulet tells Juliet about Paris – while outside, Romeo is teased by Mercutio. At the party, Tybalt recognises Romeo, but is restrained by Capulet. Romeo and Juliet meet – and part in shock: 'My only love sprung from my only hate!'

Who? What? Where? Why? How?

1   Queen Mab 1,4
2   Juliet 1, 5
3   A crutch 1,1
4   Sampson 'biting his thumb' at Abraham and Balthasar 1,1
5   In a sycamore grove west of the city 1,1
6   Because Romeo behaves well, is well spoken of in Verona, and is under Capulet's roof 1,5
7   Because she has sworn a vow of chastity 1,1
8   By his voice; because he is wearing a mask 1,5
9   Three 1,1
10 Two 1,5

Who said that?

1   Benvolio 1,1
2   Romeo 1,1
3   Mercutio 1,4
4   Capulet – repeating the general opinion of Verona 1,5
5   Tybalt 1,1

Like what?

1   The way Romeo keeps his feelings to himself 1,1
2   Juliet among other women 1,5
3   Beautiful women 1,2
4   Love 1,1

What makes you think so?

1   'Doth with their death bury their parents' strife' Prologue
2   'The fearful passage of their death-mark'd love' Prologue
3   Romeo's fear that 'this night's revels' will cause 'some vile forfeit of untimely death.' 1,4
4   Juliet's comment that 'My grave is like to be my wedding bed' 1,5

About time

1   Fourteen in two weeks' time 1,2
2   At dawn 1,1
3   Sadness 1,1
4   'We burn daylight' – since they 'waste their lights' by standing about, as much as if they kept them burning in the daytime 1,4
5   a) 'Supper is done, and we shall come too late'./'I fear too early...' (Benvolio/Romeo) 1,4
     b) 'Too early seen unknown, and known too late!' (Juliet) 1,5

Whose side?

Capulets: Juliet, Tybalt, Nurse, Peter, Sampson, Gregory – plus Paris as suitor to Juliet.

Montagues: Romeo, Abraham, Balthasar, Benvolio – plus Mercutio as a friend of Romeo.

Note: Paris and Mercutio are actually members of the Royal Family ('kinsmen of the Prince'). Obviously the Prince's family does not favour either the Montagues or the Capulets.

■ Self-test answers Act Two

Uncover the plot

Benvolio and Mercutio seek Romeo. Juliet declares her love for Romeo, who reveals himself, saying: 'I'll take thee at thy word'. Juliet is afraid that her kinsmen will kill him. They exchange vows. Romeo goes to Friar Lawrence, who is seen putting plants in a basket. He agrees to marry them because it may end the feud. Meanwhile, Tybalt has challenged Romeo to a duel. After much banter, Romeo tells the Nurse of his plan to marry Juliet and send a rope ladder to reach her later. Told the news in her turn, Juliet blushes. The lovers meet at the Friar's cell.

Who? What? Where? Why? How?

1 Tybalt 2,4
2 Mercutio 2,4
3 1) Romeo will 'deny (his) father and refuse (his) name' or 2) she will 'no longer be a Capulet' 2,2
4 'Stony limits' (Juliet's wall – later, perhaps, the tomb) 2,2
5 Why – not 'where'! She is saying: why did you have to be Romeo – a Montague? 2,2
6 To swear by himself (If he must swear) – but not by the changeable moon 2,2
7 To church, for confession and absolution ('shrift') 2,5
8 In the orchard below Juliet's room 2,2
9 For 'doting' on – not for 'loving' – Rosaline 2,3
10 Delicately and technically, like a musician 2,4

Who said that?

1 Juliet 2,2
2 Friar Lawrence 2,3
3 Mercutio 2,4
4 Romeo 2,6
5 Nurse 2,5

Open quotes

1 'But passion lends them power, time means, to meet,/Temp'ring extremities with extreme sweet.' Prologue
2 'But soft! What light through yonder window breaks?/It is the east, and Juliet is the sun.' 2,2
3 'For this alliance may so happy prove/To turn your households' rancour to pure love.' 2,3
4 'Had she affections and warm youthful blood,/She would be swift in motion as a ball.' 2,5
5 'These violent delights have violent ends,/And in their triumph die.' 2,6

About time

1 Because 'It is too rash, too unadvis'd, too sudden.' 2,2
2 'Wisely and slow; they stumble that run fast.' 2,3 and 'Too swift arrives as tardy as too slow.' 2,6
3 At nine o'clock; 20 years 2,2
4 Half an hour; three hours 2,5

Looking forward to the end?

1 Mercutio has never known the pain of love. Mercutio will die in a duel
2 Romeo would rather be killed by Juliet's kinsmen in the orchard than suffer a 'lingering death' pining for her. Romeo will in fact suffer a lingering death (by poison) in the belief that he has lost Juliet
3 If Romeo were a bird, Juliet would smother him with love. Love for Juliet will in fact be the cause of Romeo's death
4 Friar Lawrence had told Romeo to 'kill' his infatuation for Rosaline. Romeo will see his true love buried 'in a grave'
5 Romeo and Mercutio are having a 'duel' of words. It is Romeo 'coming between' Mercutio and Tybalt in a duel that causes Mercutio's death
6 Juliet thinks old people are slow and cold. It is Juliet herself who will 'feign death'
7 Friar Lawrence says only 'moderate' love lasts long. Romeo and Juliet's love is not moderate – and will be tragically brief

■ Self-test answers Act Three

Uncover the plot

Tybalt, looking to fight Romeo, instead kills Mercutio when Romeo tries to intervene, but is then killed by an enraged Romeo, who is sentenced to banishment. Juliet, distraught, sheds tears over Romeo's banishment. Romeo is told of his fate by Friar Lawrence: they are joined by the Nurse and make plans for Romeo to escape to Mantua. Capulet and Paris plan the wedding for Thursday. Meanwhile Romeo and Juliet part at dawn, on hearing a lark. Juliet is told of the wedding plan by Lady Capulet, and refuses: her father threatens to disown her. Let down even by the Nurse, Juliet is left only with the last resort of death.

Who? What? Why? How?

1 Romeo – because in Juliet's mind, at this point, he looks harmless, but has killed Tybalt 3,2
2 Friar Lawrence, the Nurse – Juliet is sarcastic, saying 'thou hast comforted me marvellous much' 3,4
3 'Banished' 3,2
4 To tell of the marriage, to reconcile his friends, to beg the Prince's pardon, to call Romeo back 3,3
5 Because Tybalt is dead and Romeo lives 3,5
6 Because Romeo says he is willing to stay – and die – if she wants him to 3,5
7 Because – unknown to Tybalt – they are now related by marriage 3,1
8 Because Juliet is alive, Tybalt is dead and Romeo is only exiled 3,3
9 By 'speaking fair', and by pleading the triviality of the quarrel and the Prince's displeasure 3,1
10 The lark (said to be a nightingale), and first light (said to be a meteor or moonglow) 3,5

Who said that?

1 The Prince 3,1
2 Benvolio 3,1
3 Mercutio – because Romeo is refusing to fight Tybalt 3,1
4 Lady Capulet of Juliet, because she refuses to be married to Paris 3,5
5 Nurse 3,5

Open quotes

1 '"Romeo is banished" – to speak that word/Is father, mother, Tybalt, Romeo, Juliet/All slain, all dead!' 3,2
2 'Yet "banished"? Hang up philosophy: unless philosophy can make a Juliet,/Displant a town, reverse a prince's doom/It helps not, it prevails not.' 3,3
3 'Is there no pity sitting in the clouds/That sees into the bottom of my grief?' 3,5
4 'O God, I have an ill-divining soul!/Methinks I see thee, now thou art below,/As one dead in the bottom of a tomb.' 3,5'
5 'More light and light it grows!'/'More light and light; more dark and dark our woes!' 3,5

Looking forward to the end?

1 Juliet wants Romeo to come back soon. He will come back – too soon, and to his death 3,5
2 Romeo's descent to the garden reminds Juliet of the grave. The next time she sees him, he will be dead in the Capulet vault 3,5
3 Juliet is saying – unbeknownst to her mother – that she would save Romeo. It is she who will sleep instead of dying – and Romeo will die of poison

Till death do us part

1 'And death, not Romeo, take my maidenhead.' 3,2
2 '...make the bridal bed/In that dim monument where Tybalt lies' 3,5
3 'I would the fool were married to her grave.' 3,5
4 'Thou art wedded to calamity' 3,3

■ Self-test answers Act Four

Uncover the plot

Paris is at Friar Lawrence's cell, informing him that the wedding is now to be on Thursday. Juliet comes to plead for help, saying she will stab herself rather than marry Paris. The Friar gives her a 'vial' or bottle, containing a substance which will make her appear dead for 42 hours, after which she will awake in the Capulet vault, to be met by Romeo. Juliet agrees to marry Paris, to the delight of her father, who advances the wedding again to Wednesday. Alone, Juliet takes the potion, with a dagger by her side. The family mourn her 'death', restrained by the knowing figure of Friar Lawrence.

Who? What? Why?

1 The bridegroom (Paris) 4,1; the Nurse 4,4
2 Cold, stiffness, stopping of breath and pulse, pallor, closed eyes 4,1
3 Capulet thinks Juliet's grief for Tybalt harmful 4,1
4 'Go home, be merry, give consent to marry Paris.' 4,1
5 She will be dressed in her best robes and carried on an open bier to the Capulet vault 4,1

6   Romeo will be informed by letter, come to Verona, wait with the Friar and take Juliet to Mantua 4,1
7   The potion may not work or may be poison; she may wake early and suffocate or be driven mad by fear 4,3
8   Because she has 'the strength of will' to kill herself rather than marry Paris 4,1
9   Because of lighter episodes before and after, and the audience's knowledge that Juliet is not dead. Because the real tragic scene is still to come 4,5
10 Because on her wedding night she won't get much sleep! 4,5

Who said that?
1   Paris 4,1
2   Juliet 4,3
3   Lady Capulet 4,5
4   Friar Lawrence 4,5
5   Nurse 4,5

About time
1   The second cock has crowed, the curfew bell has rung, Capulet says it is three o'clock 4,4
2   Capulet says: 'I'll have this knot knit up tomorrow morning.' 4,2
3   She says: 'We shall be short in our provision; 'Tis now near night.' 4,2
4   Five times
5   He says: 'Uncomfortable time, why cam'st thou now/To murder, murder our solemnity?' 4,5

Looking forward to the end?
1   This is just what happens – although Juliet has to use Romeo's dagger in the end
2   In fact, Juliet will wake too late to save Romeo – and will in fact kill herself
3   Capulet's real son-in-law and heir is Romeo – who will be dead when they first 'meet'

The seeds of truth?
1   Ties up with the 'nipping of the bud' as an image of early, wasteful death – with the irony that this death is not 'untimely', because not yet real 4,5
2   'Green' in the sense of freshly, lately buried – but it is also an image of festering and horror 4,3
3   The unnatural suggestion of 'shrieking' and violence – plus the reference to herbs and potions 4,3
4   A burial plant – recalling its association with the name of Romeo in Act 2 Sc 4
5   Enhances the contrast of 'bridal' and 'burial' – both occasions for flowers 4,5
6   The rose associated with health and beauty. The irony is that Romeo, not knowing about this pallor, will later not recognise the roses in Juliet's cheeks as a sign that she is about to wake 4,1

■ Self-test answers Act Five

Uncover the plot
Balthasar arrives in Mantua with news of Juliet's death. Romeo seeks out an apothecary to buy a poison. Meanwhile, Friar Lawrence learns that his messenger Friar John has not got through. Paris is at the vault when Romeo arrives, tries to

arrest him, and is killed. Wondering that Juliet looks so fair, Romeo poisons himself. Friar Lawrence arrives too late. Juliet, finding Romeo dead, kills herself with his dagger. Montague and Capulet are reconciled, with the pledge of a 'statue in pure gold' as a final tribute to the lovers.

Who? What? Where? When? Why?

1 Balthasar, Friar Lawrence and Paris' page 5,3
2 Capulet 5,3
3 She has died of grief at Romeo's banishment 5,3
4 That Juliet has found him dead and revived him – but he will find her 'dead', and though she will be revived, he kills himself 5,1
5 To write again to Mantua, meanwhile hiding Juliet in his cell 5,2
6 In Verona, because his companion friar had been visiting the sick and both were quarantined for being infectious 5,2
7 Three hours 5,2. One minute 5,3.
8 Because he hears the watch coming 5,3
9 Out of grief for Tybalt's death 5,3
10 The man is obviously poor and desperate: selling poison is punishable by death in Mantua 5,1

Who said that?

1 Romeo – because he can't trust the dream: there is only bad news ahead 5,1
2 Romeo 5,3
3 Paris, because he thinks Romeo is avenging himself on Juliet's body: in fact, love conquers vengeance only through the death of the lovers 5,3
4 The Prince 5,3

Open quotes

1 'A greater power than we can contradict/Hath thwarted our intents.' 5,3
2 'There is thy gold – worse poison to men's souls.' 5,1
3 'Death, that hath suck'd the honey of thy breath/Hath had no power upon thy beauty.' 5,3
4 'See what a scourge is laid upon your hate/That heaven finds means to kill your joys with love.' 5,3

Parallel lines

1 'This do I drink to thee' (as Juliet drinks the potion) 4,3
2 'Thus with a kiss I die', 'I will kiss thy lips;/Haply some poison yet doth hang on them' (Juliet) 5,3
3 'make the bridal bed in that dim monument where Tybalt lies' 3,5
4 'star-cross'd lovers' (Prologue/Chorus), 'and when he shall die,/Take him and cut him out in little stars' 3,1
5 'He that hath the steerage of my course,/Direct my sail!' (Romeo) 1,4

Notes